Penguin Education

Penguin Functional English
Second Impact

Peter Watcyn-Jones

Penguin Functional English

Second Impact

With line drawings by David Lock

Penguin Books Ltd, Harmondsworth, Middlesex, England
Penguin Books, 625 Madison Avenue, New York, New York 10022, U.S.A.
Penguin Books Australia Ltd, Ringwood, Victoria, Australia
Penguin Books Canada Ltd, 2801 John Street, Markham, Ontario, Canada L3R 1B4
Penguin Books (N.Z.) Ltd, 182–190 Wairau Road, Auckland 10, New Zealand

First published as *Impact* 1979
Reprinted 1980
Revised edition published as *Second Impact* 1983

Copyright © Peter Watcyn-Jones, 1979, 1983
Line drawings copyright © David Lock, 1979

All rights reserved

Made and printed in Great Britain by
Butler & Tanner Ltd, Frome and London
Set in Monophoto Times

Except in the United States of America, this book is sold subject
to the condition that it shall not, by way of trade or otherwise, be lent,
re-sold, hired out, or otherwise circulated without the
publisher's prior consent in any form of binding or cover other than
that in which it is published and without a similar condition
including this condition being imposed on the subsequent purchaser

Contents

Unit 1: Socializing (1)   7
Unit 2: Asking For and Giving Information (1)   16
Unit 3: Finding the Way   28
Unit 4: Suggestions   37
Unit 5: Likes, Dislikes and Preferences   45
Unit 6: Invitations   62
Unit 7: Requests and Offers   74
Unit 8: Opinions   84
Unit 9: Problems and Advice   92
Unit 10: Certainty and Uncertainty   99
Unit 11: Past Regrets   108
Unit 12: Apologies and Excuses   117
Unit 13: Socializing (2)   131
Unit 14: Asking For and Giving Information (2)   148
Unit 15: Future Plans and Intentions   162
   Materials for Exercises and Role-Plays   175
   Acknowledgements   192

Unit 1:
Socializing (1)

Mr and Mrs Evans are at Liverpool Street Station. They are awaiting the arrival of a Swedish girl called Inger, who is going to be their au-pair for the next year. Although they have never met before, they have written to one another several times, and the Evanses also have a photograph of her. The train has just come in. Mr Evans goes up to someone who looks like Inger.

MR EVANS: Excuse me, are you Inger?
STUDENT: No. My name is Ulla.
MR EVANS: Oh, sorry! *[He sees another girl and is sure that it is Inger.]* Er ... Inger?
INGER: Yes?
MR EVANS: Oh, hello. I'm so pleased to meet you. I'm Mr Evans – Colin.
INGER: Oh, yes, Mr Evans. Hello.
  [They shake hands.]
MR EVANS: And this is Mrs Evans.
MRS EVANS: Hello, dear. Call me Elsie.
  [They shake hands.]
INGER: Hello. It was very kind of you and Mr Evans to meet me.
MRS EVANS: Not at all. I hope you had a good crossing.
INGER: Not too bad, thank you, but it was a bit rough last night.
MR EVANS: Yes, it usually is on the North Sea. Still, a nice cup of tea will make you feel better, won't it, Elsie?
MRS EVANS: Oh yes, you can't beat a cup of tea.
MR EVANS: Now, let me take your cases – the car's just outside the station.
INGER: Thank you very much. They are a bit heavy.
MR EVANS: Right. Shall we go, then?
  [They go out of the station.]

Liverpool Street Station

a) How to approach the person you are meeting

When you go up to someone you are supposed to be meeting and whom you have never seen before, here are some phrases you can use:

> It's (Mr Brown), isn't it?
> (Mr/Mrs/Miss Smith)?
> Excuse me, are you (Mr Thompson)?

b) How to reply

You can reply to such an approach with one of the following phrases:

> Yes, that's right.
> Yes?
> Yes, that's right. And you must be (Mr Williams).

c) How to introduce yourself

When you want to introduce yourself, here are some phrases you can use:

I'm (Charles Brown). My name's (Sally Kent).	
I'm so pleased to meet you. I've been looking forward to meeting you. So glad to meet you.	I'm (Tom Smith).

d) How to respond and reply to an introduction

When someone is introduced to you for the first time, you *both* shake hands and say:

> How do you do.   *formal*
> Hello.   *less formal*

PRACTICE 1

Work in pairs. Take turns to approach and introduce yourself to a stranger. Use the following situations (you can use your own Christian names):

1. Someone called Brown is meeting someone called Terry.
2. Someone called Lawson is meeting someone called Overton.
3. Someone called Gibson is meeting someone called O'Hara.
4. Someone called Green is meeting someone called Jones.
5. Someone called Williams is meeting someone called Richards.
6. Someone called Grey is meeting someone called Morley.

e) How to introduce someone who is with you

If there is someone with you and you wish to introduce them to the other person, here are some phrases you can use (again, people shake hands and greet one another as above):

May I introduce	my girlfriend/boyfriend, my wife/husband,	Janet/James.
And this is	my secretary, my business colleague,	Jane Smith/Tom Williams.

PRACTICE 2

Work in groups of three – A, B and C. Take turns to introduce yourself to a stranger. Then introduce the person who is with you. Person A uses the following situations. Persons B and C look at the situations on page 186.

1. Your name is Blake. You are meeting someone called Brown.
2. Your name is Watkins. You are meeting someone called Green.
3. Your name is Hollington. You are meeting someone called Owen.
4. Your name is Brent. You are meeting someone called Carroll.
5. Your name is Collins. You are meeting someone called Davies.
6. Your name is Steadman. You are meeting someone called Smooth.

f) How to make polite remarks about the journey

When you wish to make a polite remark about a person's flight or journey, here are some phrases you can use:

Did you have a good How was the		flight? trip? journey?	
Was the (trip) all right? I hope you had a pleasant (journey)?			
A	good pleasant comfortable	crossing, flight, journey,	I hope?

g) How to reply to a polite inquiry about the journey

When someone makes a polite inquiry about your flight or journey, you can reply with one of the following:

Yes,	very good indeed, quite good, fairly pleasant, pretty good,	thank you. thanks.
No,	not very good, a bit rough, rather tiring, pretty exhausting, not too good,	I'm afraid.

Unit 1: Socializing (1)

PRACTICE 3

Work in pairs. A asks the questions below. B imagines he/she is the person in the picture and makes up a suitable reply.

1. Did you have a good flight?

2. I hope you had a pleasant trip?

3. How was the journey?

4. Was the crossing all right?

5. A good flight, I hope?

6. A pleasant trip, I hope?

7. A comfortable journey, I hope?

8. A pleasant crossing, I hope?

Unit 1: Socializing (1)

h) How to suggest leaving and offering help with luggage

When you want the person to accompany you and you want to offer to help with luggage, you can use one of the following phrases:

Well,	if you'd like to follow me. shall we go, then?	I've got a (car) waiting outside.
Now,	let me take your things. let me help you carry your bags.	The (station)'s just (opposite).

i) How to reply to an offer of help

When someone suggests you accompany him/her and offers to help you carry your luggage, you can say:

Certainly. Yes, of course. Thank you.	I'm really looking forward to staying in (London).
Thank you very much. Thank you.	That's very kind of you. They are a bit heavy.
It's all right, thanks. thank you.	I can manage. They're not very heavy.

PRACTICE 4

Work in pairs, taking turns to make a suitable reply to the following:

1. Well, if you'd like to follow me. I've got a car waiting outside.
2. Well, shall we go, then? The car's just outside.
3. Now, let me take your things. It's not far to the car park.
4. Now, let me help you carry your bags. It's not very far to the Underground.
5. Well, if you'd like to follow me. We can get a taxi to my office.
6. Well, shall we go, then? We can get a bus just outside the station.

PRACTICE 5

Work in pairs or groups of three. Take it in turns to meet someone at an airport. Use your own names. Do it like this:

1. Approach the person you are meeting	Excuse me, are you ...?
2. Introduce yourself	My name's ... How do you do.
*3. Introduce the person who is with you	May I introduce ...?
4. Ask and answer questions about the journey	Did you have a good journey?
5. Suggest leaving (you can also offer to help with luggage)	Well, shall we go, then? Now, let me help you with your bags.

(NOTE: *Leave out this part if working in pairs.)

Written Practice

Complete the following dialogues with a suitable phrase:

1. A: ....?
   B: Yes, that's right. And you must be ....

2. A: .... I'm Sheila Kent.
   B: How ....
   A: ....

3. A: .... my wife, Julie.
   B: ....
   C: ....

4. A: Did you have a good flight?
   B: ....

5. A: ....?
   B: No, a bit rough, I'm afraid.

6. A: .... journey?
   B: ....

7. A: Well, ... The car's just outside.
   B: ....

8. A: Now, ... bags.
   B: ....

Unit 1: Socializing (1)

Dialogue

Practise reading the following dialogue in groups of three. Read the dialogue again, replacing the phrases in **bold** with phrases of similar meaning. Then write out the new dialogue.

A: Excuse me.

B: Yes?

A: **It's Mr Gibson, isn't it?**

B: **Yes, that's right.**

A: **So glad to meet you. I'm** Simon Steel. *[They shake hands.]* **How do you do.**

B: **How do you do.** It was nice of you to meet us.

A: It's a pleasure.

B: **And this is** my wife, Sally.

   [They shake hands.]

C: **How do you do,** Mr Steel.

A: **How do you do. Did you have a good** flight?

C: Yes, **pretty good, thanks.** But I must say I don't think I'll ever get used to flying.

A: Well, **if you'd like to follow me.** I've got a car waiting outside.

B: Yes, **certainly.** Thank you.

A: Now, **let me help you with your bags,** Mrs Gibson.

C: **Thank you. They are a bit heavy.**

A: Right. This way. It's not very far.

Role-Play

MEETING SOMEONE AT AN AIRPORT

Work in groups of up to twelve students.

This role-play is all about meeting someone for the first time at an airport. Some of the class will be those waiting to meet someone, while the rest will be those who are being met.

Before you start, the people meeting someone choose a role from those on pages 175–6 and the people being met choose a role from those on pages 176–7.

When you have done it once, change roles and do it again.

Unit 2: Asking For and Giving Information (1)

Simon Watson is at a party. He sees a girl standing alone in the corner of the room. He has never seen her before. He decides to go over and talk to her.

SIMON: Hello. May I join you?
JOANNA: Yes, of course.
SIMON: Quite a good party, isn't it?
JOANNA: Yes, very good.
   [a slight pause]
SIMON: Do you smoke?
JOANNA: No, I don't, actually.
SIMON: Lucky you! I wish I didn't have to. *[He takes out a cigarette and lights it.]* By the way, I'm Simon ... Simon Watson.
JOANNA: Oh, hello. My name's Jo.
SIMON: Joe? That's a boy's name, isn't it?
JOANNA: No, it's short for Joanna, actually.
SIMON: Oh, sorry.
JOANNA: That's all right.
SIMON: Where are you from?
JOANNA: Scotland. From Edinburgh, actually.
SIMON: Are you here on holiday or something?
JOANNA: No, on business, as a matter of fact. I'm looking for a flat in London.
SIMON: I see. So I don't suppose you know many of the people here, then?
JOANNA: No, hardly anyone.
SIMON: Not to worry ... the night's still young. *[He smiles. A short pause. The record changes. A lively rock-and-roll song comes on.]* You do dance, don't you?
JOANNA: Yes, of course.
SIMON: Well, this sounds lively. Would you like to try it?
JOANNA: Yes, all right.
SIMON: Good.
   [They start dancing.]

Edinburgh Castle

a) How to ask and answer direct questions where a short Yes or No answer is expected

When you ask someone a direct question and expect a short Yes or No answer, here are some of the most common types of questions used.

You can ask: answer:

Are you	cold? waiting for someone? coming on Friday?	Yes, I am./ No, I'm not.
Is	your sister with you? it raining? your brother married?	Yes, (he) is./ No, (it) isn't.
Are there	any rooms to let? any questions you'd like to ask?	Yes, there are./ No, there aren't.
Is there	a station near here? time to buy a newspaper?	Yes, there is./ No, there isn't.
Were you	late this morning? born in England? ill on Friday?	Yes, I was./ No, I wasn't.
Was	your brother with you last night? it cold this morning? your mother angry with you?	Yes, (he) was./ No, (it) wasn't.
Were there	many people at the party? any problems?	Yes, there were./ No, there weren't.
Was there	a lot of traffic this morning? anyone there you knew?	Yes, there was./ No, there wasn't.
Can	you swim? you come back tomorrow? your sister play tennis?	Yes, (I) can./ No, (she) can't.
Have you	(got) any cigarettes? told him yet? ever been to Paris?	Yes, I have./ No, I haven't.

Has	your brother (got) a car? it stopped raining yet? Mrs Collins arrived?	Yes, (he) has./ No, (it) hasn't.
Do you	come from France? speak English? live in a flat?	Yes, I do./ No, I don't.
Does	your wife play bridge? this pen belong to you? he know you're here?	Yes, (she) does./ No, (it) doesn't.
Did you	see him yesterday? like the play? go away last summer?	Yes, I did./ No, I didn't.
Did	it rain last night? your brother go with you? he tell you to wait here?	Yes, (it) did./ No, (he) didn't.

PRACTICE 1

Work in pairs. A asks direct questions, using the words below. B gives a short Yes or No answer.

Ask B if:

1. he/she is English.
2. it's cold today.
3. there are any mountains in his/her country.
4. there's a swimming-pool near here.
5. he/she was born in England.
6. it was warm yesterday.
7. there were any good programmes on TV last night.
8. there was a lot of traffic this morning.
9. he/she can play the guitar.
10. his/her parents can speak English.
11. he's/she's got a car.
12. he's/she's ever been to Scotland.
13. his/her mother has ever been to London.
14. he/she lives in a flat.
15. it snows a lot in his/her country.
16. he/she learnt English at school.
17. it rained last weekend.
18. he/she went out last night.

b) How to ask and answer direct questions where a more detailed answer than Yes or No is expected

When you ask someone a direct question and want a more detailed answer than Yes or No, begin your question with a question word (e.g. Why? What? etc.). Here are some questions you can ask:

What's	your name? the time? that building over there?
What	nationality are you? do you usually do at weekends? have you been doing today?
How's	your mother? he going to get home? it going?
How	do you know he lives in a flat? many people live in your country? did you get home last night?
When	do you usually start work? did you first visit England? can you see me?
How long	does it take to get to Brighton? can you stay? have you been working for the B.B.C.?
Where	do you live? did you go last night? have you put my tie?
Which	car is his? country do you come from? job did you finally take?
Why	do you want this job? are you late? did you say that to her?

Unit 2: Asking For and Giving Information (1)

Here are some ways you can answer:
(NOTE: In conversation we usually leave out the words in brackets.)

(My name's) Peter Browne. It's 10 o'clock. That's the Post Office Tower.
I'm Swedish. (I usually) stay at home and watch TV. (I've been) working hard as usual.
She's fine, thanks. (He says he's going) by taxi. Very well, thanks.
(Because) he told me. About 50 million. Oh, (I got home) by bus.
(I usually start work) at 9 o'clock. (I first visited England) in 1964. (I can see you) tomorrow afternoon, if you like.
(It takes) about an hour. Not very long, I'm afraid. (I've been working there) since 1970.
(I live) in Chelsea. (I went) to the cinema. (It's) in the top drawer.
(It's) the blue Mini over there. (I come from) France. (I finally took) the one in Scotland.
Because I've always been interested in advertising. I'm sorry, but I missed the bus. Because I felt like it – that's all!

PRACTICE 2

Work in pairs. Take turns to ask and answer direct questions, below.

Ask someone:

1. what the time is.
2. what he/she did last night.
3. what sort of books he/she likes reading.
4. how he/she is.
5. how he/she usually gets to work.
6. when he/she got up this morning.
7. when he/she first visited England.
8. how long he's/she's been learning English.
9. how long it takes him/her to get home from here.
10. where he/she lives.
11. where he/she went last summer.
12. which pop group he/she likes.
13. which country he/she comes from.
14. why he's/she's learning English.

c) How to ask a direct question when you already think you know what the answer will be

Sometimes people ask questions even though they are almost certain of what the answer will be. Here are some ways of asking questions.

When you expect a Yes answer:

> You are married, aren't you?
> You were born in Poland, weren't you?
> You can come tomorrow, can't you?
> You have got a car, haven't you?
> You do smoke, don't you?
> You did thank him, didn't you?

Asking For and Giving Information (1)

When you expect a No answer:

> You aren't cold, are you?
> You weren't ill last week, were you?
> You can't swim, can you?
> You haven't been here before, have you?
> You don't live in London, do you?
> You didn't see him last night, did you?

d) How to reply by confirming that the answer is Yes or No, i.e. giving the expected response

| Yes, (that's right,) | I am. / I was. / I can. / I have. / I do. / I did. | or | No, | I'm not. / I wasn't. / I can't. / I haven't. / I don't. / I didn't. |

e) How to reply by not confirming the person's question, i.e. giving the unexpected response

| Well, as a matter of fact | I'm not. / I wasn't. / I can't. / I haven't. / I don't. / I didn't. |

or

| Well, | I am, / I was, / I can, / I have, / I do, / I did, | actually. |

PRACTICE 3

Work in pairs. A is a reporter interviewing B, an actor. A uses the words below to ask B questions expecting a Yes or No answer. B gives the expected response, shown in brackets.

1. born in London (*Yes*)

2. a film actor (*Yes*)

3. married (*Yes*)

4. three children (*Yes*)

5. like playing football (*No*)

6. appear on TV last year (*Yes*)

7. go abroad last week (*No*)

8. planning to make a film soon (*No*)

PRACTICE 4

Repeat Practice 3, but this time B gives the unexpected response.

Unit 2: Asking For and Giving Information (1)

Written Practice 1

Write out the following questions and answer them:

1. Ask someone if he/she is cold.
   A: ....?
   B: ....

2. Ask someone if he/she can play the piano.
   A: ....?
   B: ....

3. Ask someone is he's/she's got any brothers.
   A: ....?
   B: ....

4. Ask someone if he/she likes pop music.
   A: ....?
   B: ....

5. Ask someone if there was a lot of traffic this morning.
   A: ....?
   B: ....

6. Ask someone what he/she usually has for breakfast.
   A: ....?
   B: ....

7. Ask someone where he/she was born.
   A: ....?
   B: ....

8. Ask someone how he's/she's getting home today.
   A: ....?
   B: ....

9. Ask someone when he/she first went abroad.
   A: ....?
   B: ....

10. Ask someone how long it takes to fly to America.
    A: ....?
    B: ....

11. Ask someone where he/she lives.
    A: ....?
    B: ....

12. Ask someone why he/she wanted to learn English.
    A: ....?
    B: ....

Written Practice 2

Complete the following dialogues:

1. A: You are married, ...?
   B: Yes, ...

2. A: You didn't watch TV last night, ...?
   B: No, ...

3. A: You do have a car, ...?
   B: Yes, ...

4. A: You can't swim, ...?
   B: No, ...

5. A: You have ....?
   B: Yes, ...

6. A: You don't ....?
   B: No, ...

7. A: You can play the piano, ...?
   B: Well, ..., I can't.

8. A: You don't smoke, ...?
   B: Well, ..., actually.

9. A: You did ....?
   B: Well, ...

10. A: You haven't
    B: Well, ...

Unit 2: Asking For and Giving Information (1)

Dialogue

Practise reading the following dialogue in pairs. Read the dialogue again, replacing the phrases in **bold** with phrases of similar meaning. Then write out the new dialogue.

A: So **you come from** Edinburgh, do you, Joanna?

B: Yes, **that's right.**

A: Well, it's certainly a **beautiful city.**

B: Oh, **you've been there, have you?**

A: No, **I haven't, actually.** I saw it on TV when the Festival was there. **Is there a festival** every year?

B: Yes, **there is.**

A: By the way, **where are you staying in London?**

B: The Selfridge Hotel. **Do you know it, Simon?**

A: **Oh, yes.** As a matter of fact **I've got a flat just round the corner from it.**

B: **Have you** really? Well, **isn't that** strange?

A: Yes, it is, isn't it?

B: Oh, would you excuse me for a moment? I just want to **have a word with someone.**

A: **Certainly.** But you'll dance with me later on, won't you?

B: Yes, **of course.**

  [She goes off to talk to a friend.]

Role-Play

AT A PARTY

For the whole class in pairs.

A group of new students are to start at college next week. A party has been arranged for them to meet and become acquainted with some second-year students.

The class divides into two groups, first-year students and second-year students.

The first-year students stand in various parts of the room. The second-year students enter the room and then each one individually approaches one of the first-year students, introduces himself/herself and has a short conversation.

After a while each second-year student makes an excuse to leave and goes to stand in a different part of the room. Each first-year student then approaches a second-year student.

The whole process is repeated until each student has met all the others.

Group Work

Work in groups of up to eight students.

1. Copy out one of the cards on pages 178–9 on a separate piece of paper.
2. Work out how to ask each of the six questions.
3. Now go around the class taking it in turns to ask and answer questions. If someone answers **Yes** to a question, make a note of his/her name. If nobody answers **Yes** to a question, make a note of that too. Try to talk to everyone in the group.
4. When you have finished, take it in turns to tell the group what you found out, e.g.

> **I found out that both Sven and Pierre can do a handstand. Also that nobody has ever been to Scotland ...** etc.

Unit 3:
Finding the Way

Claire and Brian are asking for directions to Castle Road where Peter and Sally Gibson live.

BRIAN: Excuse me.
WOMAN: Yes?
BRIAN: Sorry to bother you, but could you tell me the way to Castle Road, please?
WOMAN: I'm afraid I've no idea. I'm a stranger here myself.
BRIAN: Oh, I see. Well, thank you anyway.
WOMAN: Sorry I couldn't help.
[They walk on for a little while. They go up to a taxi-driver.]
CLAIRE: Excuse me.
TAXI-DRIVER: Yes?
CLAIRE: Could you tell me how to get to Castle Road, please?
TAXI-DRIVER: Castle Road? Let me think, now ... Yes ... Go along this road as far as Tesco's – that's a large supermarket – then turn left and Castle Road is the first turning on the right.
CLAIRE: I see. Straight on as far as the supermarket ... turn left ... then right.
TAXI-DRIVER: Yes, that's right.
CLAIRE: It's not too far from here, is it?
TAXI-DRIVER: Oh no, only a few minutes.
CLAIRE: Oh, good. Well, thank you very much.
TAXI-DRIVER: Not at all.
[They go off in the direction of Castle Road.]

Unit 3: Finding the Way

a) How to ask someone the way

When asking someone the way to a particular building, street, etc., you can use one of the following phrases:

Excuse me,	can could	you tell me	the way to (Foyle Road), where (the post office) is, how to get to (Green Street),	please?

b) How to say you are unable to give directions

If you yourself are asked and do not know the way, here are some phrases you can use:

I'm sorry,	I don't know. I've no idea.	(I'm a stranger here myself.)
I'm afraid	I don't know. I can't help you.	

PRACTICE 1

Work in pairs. A looks at the pictures and asks B the way to the places listed. B is a stranger in the town and replies accordingly.

1. the cinema

2. the post office

3. the police station

Unit 3: Finding the Way

4. the library

5. the station

6. the museum

7. the chemist's

8. the hospital

c) How to give simple directions

When you are asked the way to a building or a street farther along the street you are now in, you can use one of the following phrases:

Walk Go Carry on	down along up	this road/street, and it's

on the	left right	next to near opposite	the bank. the cinema. the post office. the car park. the police station.
the	first second third	turning street road	on the	right. left.
at the corner of (the High Street) and (Foyle Road).			

Unit 3: Finding the Way

PRACTICE 2

Look at the following map:

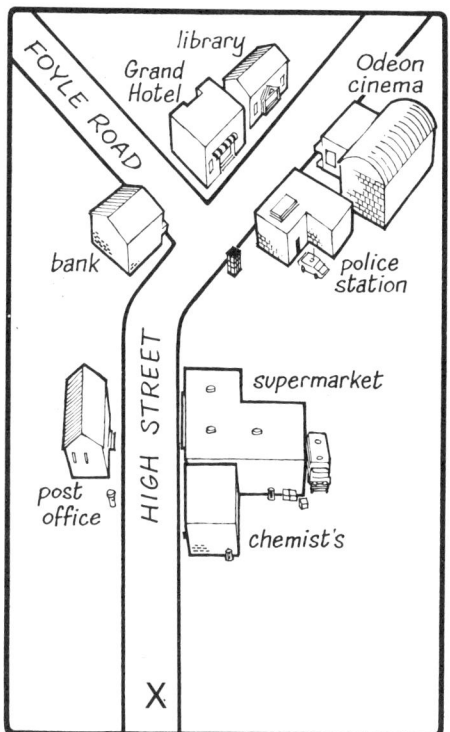

A stranger standing at point X stops and asks someone the way to the library:

> A: Excuse me.
> B: Yes?
> A: Can you tell me the way to the library, please?
> B: Certainly. Go along this street, and it's on the left, opposite the cinema.
> A: Thank you very much.
> B: Not at all.

Now, work in pairs, taking turns to ask for and give directions from point X to the following:

1. the bank
2. the Grand Hotel
3. Foyle Road
4. the post office
5. the police station
6. the chemist's
7. the Odeon cinema
8. the supermarket

Unit 3: Finding the Way

d) How to give more complex directions

When someone asks you the way to a building, street, etc., and it is in, or off, a different street from the one in which you are now standing, you can use the following phrases:

Go straight	up down	this	road street
Go along			

until you	come get	to a	post office. set of traffic lights. church.
as far as the			crossroads. pub. roundabout.

Then turn	left right	into at	(Harold Road). (Green Street). (Cherry Avenue).
		at the (next)	crossroads. junction. set of traffic lights. post office, etc.

Then take the	first second third	turning road	on the	left. right.
Then turn (left), then (right).				

And it's at the end of	the that	road, on the	left. right.

e) How to give an idea of distance

It's	not (very) far. only about (5 minutes) from here. quite near here (actually).	
It won't take you very long It'll only take about (10 minutes)		to get there.

Unit 3: Finding the Way

PRACTICE 3

Look at the following map:

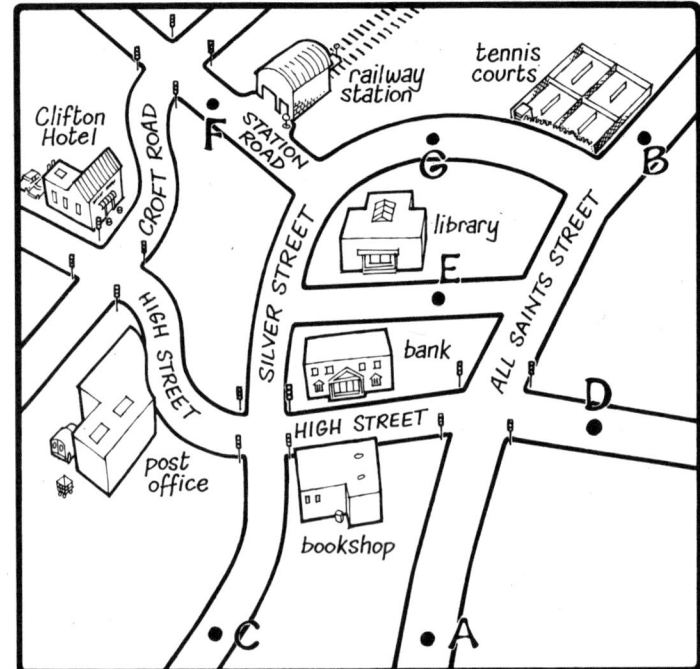

A stranger standing at point A asks the way to the bank:

A: Excuse me.
B: Yes?
A: Could you tell me how to get to the bank, please?
B: Yes, of course. Go along this road as far as the traffic lights. Then turn left into the High Street and it's on the right.
A: Is it far?
B: No, not very far.
A: Thank you very much.
B: You're welcome.

Now, work in pairs, taking turns to ask for and give directions for the following:

A stranger standing at point:

1. B wants to get to the library.
2. C wants to get to the post office.
3. D wants to get to the tennis courts.
4. E wants to get to the railway station.
5. F wants to get to the Clifton Hotel.
6. G wants to get to the bookshop.

PRACTICE 4

Work in pairs. Using the map below, go through the following situations, taking it in turns to ask for and give directions:

1. You are standing outside the library in London Road (East). You are supposed to meet some friends at The Swan pub, but you don't know where it is. Stop someone and ask him/her the way.
2. You have stopped for petrol at the garage in Cambridge Road. You have come to visit your sister who lives in Church Lane. Ask the garage attendant the way.
3. You are standing outside the school in School Lane. You want to post a letter. Ask one of the pupils where the nearest post office is.
4. You have just arrived at Anytown and are standing outside the railway station. You have come to visit your aunt who is in hospital. Ask someone how to get there.
5. Your car has broken down near the library in Sheep Street. You want to phone a garage. Ask someone where the nearest telephone kiosk is.

Anytown

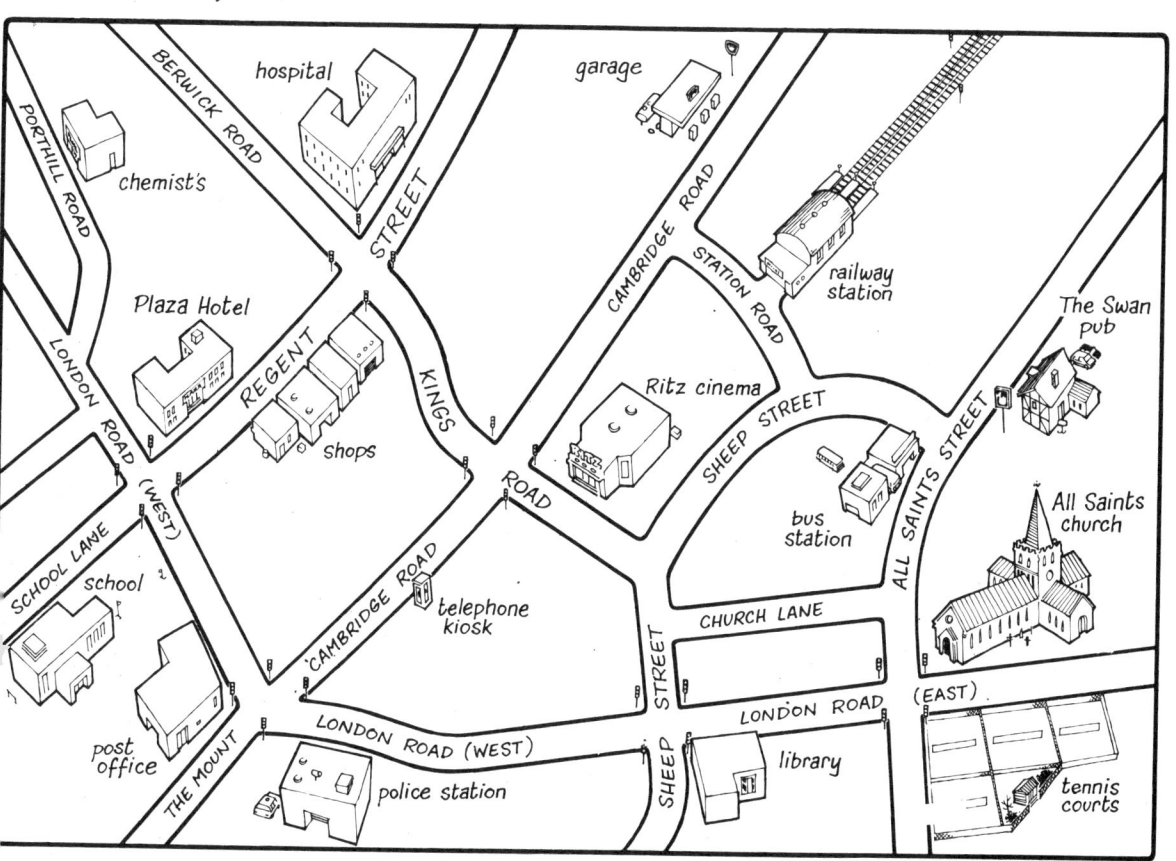

Unit 3: Finding the Way

Role-Play

Work in pairs. Person A reads through the situations below, while Person B reads through the situations on page 186. Do this now!

SITUATION 1

You work at the library in Anytown. Person B has applied for a job there and phones you up to ask you how to get there from the station. Give him/her clear directions using the map of Anytown on the previous page.
(NOTE: Person B has a map but the only things that are marked on it are the railway station, All Saints church and London Road (East) and London Road (West).

SITUATION 2

You are standing outside All Saints church opposite the tennis courts when a stranger (Person B) asks you the way to the hospital. Give him/her clear directions how to get there, using the map of Anytown on the previous page.
(NOTE: Person B has a map but the only things that are marked on it are the railway station, All Saints church, London Road (East) and London Road (West).

Unit 4: Suggestions

Sally is at home watching television with Peter. It is Friday evening.

SALLY: Do you feel like doing anything tomorrow evening, Peter?
PETER: Yes, all right. What do you suggest?
SALLY: How about going to see *Star Wars*? It's on locally and they say it's very good.
PETER: Well, we could, I suppose, but I don't really like science-fiction films all that much. Of course, if you'd like to see it ...
SALLY: No, no ... I don't mind. It was just a suggestion, that's all.
   [A slight pause. They continue watching television.]
PETER: We could always go to Dave's party, I suppose.
SALLY: Dave?
PETER: Yes, Dave Wilkins. You know – that chap who works for the B.B.C. He's having a sort of house-warming party. Everyone's invited. So if you fancy going, then we ...
SALLY: No, I don't think so somehow! You know what Dave's parties are like. I still haven't recovered from the last one we went to.
PETER: Well, it was only an idea.
SALLY: No, I'd prefer to go somewhere else, if you don't mind. Just the two of us.
PETER: Would you like to go for a meal, then? We could go to that new French restaurant in Chelsea. Brian told me the food was really great.
SALLY: Yes, that would be nice. Let's do that. And why don't we call in on Bob and Sue on the way home? We've been promising to go and see them for ages.
PETER: Yes, good idea. We could even go on to Dave's party afterwards.
SALLY: Peter! If you think I'm going ...
PETER: *[laughing]* It's all right. I'm only joking!

Unit 4: Suggestions

a) How to ask for a suggestion

When you ask someone to suggest something, here are some phrases you can use:

What	shall we do you suggest we would you like to do you want to can we	do tonight?
Where	do you fancy	going at the weekend?

b) How to make a suggestion

When you make a suggestion, here are some phrases you can use:

What about How about Do you fancy Do you feel like	going to the pictures?
Shall we Let's Why don't we Why not I suggest we Would you like to	spend the weekend in Brighton(?)

PRACTICE 1

Match up the requests from A with an appropriate suggestion from B.

A
> What do you fancy eating tonight?
> Where do you want to go tonight?
> Who do you suggest we invite to the party?
> What can we do at the weekend?
> Where shall we go for our holidays?
> When would you like to visit your cousin in Wales?

38

Unit 4: Suggestions

B
Let's go and stay with my sister in Brighton.
How about a nice curry?
Why don't we ask our English teacher?
I suggest we go and see her at Easter.
Why not go to the pub?
What about going to Spain?

PRACTICE 2

Work in pairs. A makes up a question using the following prompts. B answers with an appropriate suggestion.

A asks:

1. where/go tonight.
2. what/do at the weekend.
3. which film/go and see.
4. what/eat tonight.
5. when/go and see the new James Bond film.
6. who/invite to the party.

c) How to accept a suggestion

Yes,	good idea.
	that's a marvellous idea.
	that would be nice.
	that seems all right.

d) How to half-accept a suggestion

Well,	we could,	I suppose,	but (there aren't any good films on at the moment).
	that's a good idea,		
	it's not a bad idea,		
Yes, I suppose we could,			

39

Unit 4: Suggestions

e) How to reject a suggestion

No,	I can't. I don't think so. I don't think I can. I don't really feel like (going to the pictures).
Well,	I'm not sure. I don't really like (curry) very much. I'd rather not, if you don't mind.

f) How to make a counter-suggestion

Well,	I'd rather I think I'd prefer to	(go to the pub),	if you don't mind. if that's all right with you.
Mmm, but wouldn't you		prefer to rather	(go dancing)?

PRACTICE 3

Match up the suggestions from A with the most appropriate response from B.

A
What about going for a walk?
Shall we watch *Coronation Street* tonight?
Let's get married next weekend.
How about having a party on Friday?
Why not go to Majorca in the summer?
Do you fancy going to a Chinese restaurant tonight?

B
I'm not sure. I don't really like Chinese food very much.
Mmm, but wouldn't you prefer to go to Scotland again?
Well, I'd rather not, if you don't mind.
I can't. I'm already married.
Well, I think I'd prefer to watch the serial, if that's all right with you.
Well, we could, I suppose, but remember we've got to get up early on Saturday morning.

PRACTICE 4

Work in pairs. A looks at the pictures and makes a suggestion. B answers by accepting, half-accepting, rejecting or making a counter-suggestion.

1. on Saturday
2. tonight 
3. in the summer 
4. at the weekend 
5. tomorrow night 
6. tonight 

Written Practice

Complete the following dialogues:

1. A: Where shall we go tonight?
   B: What about ....
   A: Yes, ...

2. A: What do you suggest I wear to the party?
   B: How about ....
   A: No, ...

3. A: .... at the weekend?
   B: Why don't we ....?
   A: Well, ..., but ....

4. A: When .... visit Tom and Alice?
   B: Let's ....
   A: Well, I'd rather ....

5. A: Where ....?
   B: .... Spain?
   A: ....

6. A: ....?
   B: ....
   A: Yes, I suppose we could, but it's always so crowded on Saturdays.

Unit 4: Suggestions

Dialogue

Practise reading the following dialogue in pairs. Read the dialogue again, replacing the phrases in **bold** with phrases of similar meaning. Then write out the new dialogue.

A: What **shall we** do tonight?

B: **Why don't we** go to the cinema?

A: **Well, we could, I suppose,** but there aren't really any good films on at the moment.

B: Well, what **do you suggest,** then?

A: **How about** going to see Paul and Jenny?

B: **No, I don't really fancy** that.

A: All right. **Do you feel like** going to the club, then?

B: **Well, I think I'd prefer to** go dancing.

A: That's O.K. by me. And **why not** go on to a restaurant afterwards?

B: Yes, **that's a marvellous idea.**

Unit 4: Suggestions

Role-Play

GOING SOMEWHERE AT THE WEEKEND

Work in pairs or groups of three.

You want to go somewhere this weekend. Look at the Weekend Guide on page 44 and try to decide where to go.

PAIRS

Before you start, look at the notes on page 183 (Person A) and page 187 (Person B).

GROUPS OF THREE

Before you start, look at the notes on page 183 (Person A), page 187 (Person B) and page 191 (Person C).

Weekend Guide

EXHIBITIONS

IDEAL HOME EXHIBITION

See the latest designs in kitchens, bedrooms, furniture etc. Town Hall. Mon.–Sun. 10 a.m.–6 p.m.

TOWARDS THE YEAR 2000

The latest from the world of electronics. Micro-computers, videos, electronic games etc. Trade Centre. Mon.–Sun. 10.30 a.m.–4.30 p.m.

PRESS PHOTOGRAPHS

Selection of award-winning photographs from local and national newspapers. Local library. Sat. 10 a.m.–5 p.m.

COACH TOURS

WINDSOR SAFARI PARK

Come to Windsor Safari Park and Dolphinarium this weekend. New this year – prehistoric forest. Also water-skiing dolphins from the U.S.A. Coach leaves: Sat. 8 a.m. Sun. 8.30 a.m.

STONEHENGE, BATH AND LONGLEAT HOUSE

The tour visits Stonehenge on Salisbury Plain, then goes on to Longleat House, the home of the Marquess of Bath. Stop for lunch. Then on to Bath, one of Britain's most famous Georgian cities. Sat. and Sun. Coach leaves 7.30 a.m.

SPORTING EVENTS

MOTOR-RACING

International motor-racing at Brent's Head. Sat. and Sun. 11 a.m.

SHOW JUMPING

County championships at Priory Farm. Competitors include Princess Anne and Captain Mark Phillips. Dance in the evening. Sat.–Sun. 10 a.m.–3.30 p.m.

ATHLETICS

International athletics meeting at Gower Stadium. England v. West Germany. Sat. 10 a.m.–7.30 p.m.

WOMEN'S FOOTBALL MATCH

Charity football match between two women's teams – a Show-Biz XI and a TV XI at the Grove Field. Sat. Kick-off 3.30 p.m.

OTHER EVENTS

BILLIARDS CHAMPIONSHIP

National billiards championship at the Conservative Club. Fri.–Sun. 10 a.m.–6 p.m.

GRAND AUCTION

Auction at the Grand Hotel. Everything must go! Lots of bargains. Sat.–Sun. 10.30 a.m.–5 p.m.

DOG SHOW

Local dog show at Netherfield Hall. Sat. 10 a.m.–6 p.m. Judging of 'Best Dog' at 4.30 p.m. Refreshments available.

CIRCUS

Chippendale's Circus at Barclay Common. Tues.–Sun. Performances daily: 2 p.m., 5 p.m. and 7.30 p.m.

Unit 5:
Likes, Dislikes and Preferences

Sally is sitting in a café with Lorraine, a friend from work. It is raining heavily outside.

SALLY: I hate winters in England, I really do! It's always raining. We hardly ever get any snow, do we?

LORRAINE: No, thank goodness!

SALLY: Why? Don't you like snow then, Lorraine?

LORRAINE: Like it? I can't stand it! And neither would you if you had to drive to work every day as I do.

SALLY: Well, I wouldn't know about that. But you can't like this sort of weather, surely?

LORRAINE: I don't mind it, really. And I definitely prefer it to snow – especially in a city. All the slush everywhere. I don't see how anyone could enjoy walking around in that.

SALLY: Still, summer'll soon be here. Then it's Italy and all that sunshine. Lovely!

LORRAINE: You like Italy, don't you?

SALLY: Oh, I love it! Peter and I go there every summer. You ought to come with us some time, Lorraine. I'm sure you'd really enjoy it very much.

LORRAINE: No, thanks. I'm not very keen on lying on the beach all day. I prefer a more active sort of holiday.

SALLY: Such as?

LORRAINE: Well, I was thinking of going camping somewhere – Scotland maybe.

SALLY: Camping? Oh, I don't see how you can like that! All the fuss and bother every day putting up a tent. And Scotland? What if it rains? You're stuck in a tent all day.

LORRAINE: Perhaps, but I don't mind that. I always take some books with me to read. And anyway, I'd much prefer to be stuck in a tent on a mountain in Scotland than on a crowded beach in Italy, I can tell you!

SALLY: Well, rather you than me, Lorraine. All I know is that I tried camping once and loathed every minute of it. And camping sites are often as crowded as beaches!

Unit 5: Likes, Dislikes and Preferences

a) How to express likes

When talking about your likes, you can use the following words and phrases:

I	(quite)	like enjoy		jazz. French food.
I	(really)	like enjoy love		cooking. dancing. football.
I'm	(rather) (very) (extremely)		fond of keen on	parties. music. jogging.

b) How to agree or disagree with a person's likes

Agreeing:

Do you?	So do I. Me too.
Are you? So am I. Yes, me too.	
Yes, I like (dancing) too.	

Disagreeing:

Do you? I don't. Oh, I don't.
Are you? I'm not. Oh, I'm not.
Oh, I don't like (French food) at all.

Unit 5: Likes, Dislikes and Preferences

PRACTICE 1

Work in pairs. A imagines he/she likes the subjects illustrated below, and expresses his/her liking. B agrees or disagrees accordingly.

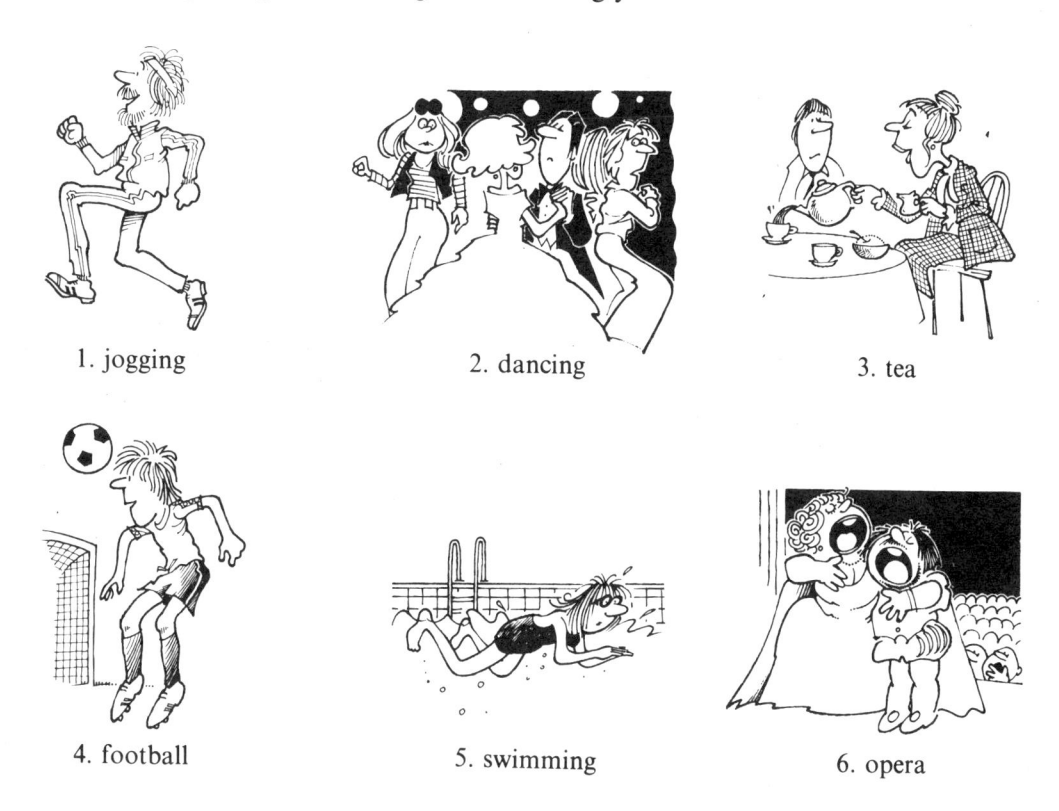

1. jogging
2. dancing
3. tea
4. football
5. swimming
6. opera

c) How to express dislikes

When talking about your dislikes, you can use the following words and phrases:

I	don't like	people who smoke. Chinese food. watching TV.
	dislike hate detest loathe	
	can't stand can't bear	

47

Unit 5: Likes, Dislikes and Preferences

d) How to agree or disagree with a person's dislikes

Agreeing:

No,	neither do I. nor do I.
No, I don't like (Chinese food) either.	
Yes,	so do I. me too.
Yes, I hate (people who smoke), too.	
No,	neither can I. nor can I. I can't (stand them) either.

Disagreeing:

Don't you? I do.   Oh, I do. I love (people who smoke).
Do you? I don't.   Oh, I don't. I love (watching TV).
Can't you? Oh, I don't mind (people who smoke) at all/ one bit.

PRACTICE 2

Work in pairs. A imagines he/she dislikes the subjects illustrated below, and expresses his/her dislikes. B agrees or disagrees accordingly. Try to use as many different phrases as possible.

1. hitch-hiking
2. singing
3. coffee
4. Chinese food

5. walking
6. London
7. driving
8. pop music

e) How to ask about particular likes and dislikes

Do you like	large cars? watching TV? French food? sunshine?
Are you fond of	rain? dancing? reading? going to parties?

and how to answer:

Yes,	I do. I am. very much. I love it/them. I quite like it/them.

No,	I don't. I'm not. not very much. not really/particularly. not at all. I hate it/them. I can't stand it/them.

PRACTICE 3

Work in pairs. Look at the topics in Practice 1 and Practice 2 and take turns to ask and answer questions about your likes and dislikes.

f) How to ask how a person likes/dislikes spending time

What	don't you like		doing in your spare time?
	do you	like enjoy dislike hate detest loathe	
	are you	fond of keen on	

Unit 5: Likes, Dislikes and Preferences

How to answer:

I	like enjoy love dislike hate detest loathe	motor-racing. skiing. painting. cooking huge meals. travelling.
I'm	fond of keen on	

Unit 5: Likes, Dislikes and Preferences

PRACTICE 4

Work in pairs. Take turns to ask and answer questions about your likes and dislikes using the following sentences and filling in the blanks.

   e.g. 1. What *do you loathe doing* at weekends?

Ask:
1. What .... at weekends?
2. Where .... at Christmas?
3. What .... for breakfast?
4. When................ getting up in the mornings?
5. Where .... for your holidays?
6. Who .... being with?
7. Why .... studying languages?
8. What .... watching on TV?

Unit 5: Likes, Dislikes and Preferences

g) How to ask about types of likes and dislikes

You can ask:

What	sort of kind of type of	books clothes films music food	do you	like? dislike?
Who	is are	your (least) favourite		author(s)? pop group(s)?

and answer:

Well, I	like don't like	science fiction jeans Westerns pop music Indian food	(very much).	
That's a difficult question, but			possibly perhaps	Thomas Hardy. Abba.
My (least) favourite	author? pop group?		Oh, without doubt	Thomas Hardy. Abba.
Oh,	Thomas Hardy, Abba,	of course.		

PRACTICE 5

Work in pairs. Take turns to ask and answer questions about your likes and dislikes. Use the following words:

1. What sort of music. . . . . ?
2. What kind of car . . . . ?
3. What type of clothes . . . . ?
4. What sort of food . . . . ?
5. . . . . (least) favourite author?
6. . . . . (least) favourite football team?
7. . . . . (least) favourite singer?
8. . . . . (least) favourite actor/actress?

Unit 5: Likes, Dislikes and Preferences

Written Practice 1

Complete the following dialogues:

1. A: I really .... playing football.
   B: .... (*disagrees*)

2. A: I .... women who use too much make-up.
   B: .... (*agrees*)

3. A: Do you like ....?
   B: .... (*says Yes*)

4. A: Do you hate ....?
   B: .... (*says No*)

5. A: What do you like doing in your spare time?
   B: ....
   A: .... (*agrees*)

6. A: What .... books do you like?
   B: ....
   A: .... (*disagrees*)

7. A: What .... clothes do you hate wearing?
   B: ....
   A: .... (*agrees*)

h) How to express preferences

When talking about your preferences, you can use the following words and phrases:

I	(much) (always)	prefer	apples	to	oranges.
			watching TV		listening to records.
I'd (much)		prefer to rather	go to the cinema	than	(go) to the theatre.

53

Unit 5: Likes, Dislikes and Preferences

i) How to agree or disagree with a person's preferences

Agreeing:

Do you?	So do I. / Me too.
Yes, I prefer (apples), too.	
Would you? So would I.	
Yes, I'd	prefer to / rather

go to the cinema, too.

Disagreeing:

Do you? I don't.
Oh, I don't. I much prefer going to the theatre.

Would you? I wouldn't.
Oh, I wouldn't. I'd much rather/prefer to go to the theatre.

Well, personally,	I like them both equally well. / I don't like either.

PRACTICE 6

Work in pairs. A expresses his/her preferences, using the words below. B agrees or disagrees accordingly. Try to use as many different phrases as possible, and change the verb where necessary.

1. watch TV *or* listen to the radio
2. go to bed early *or* late
3. read detective stories *or* science fiction
4. large cars *or* small cars
5. tomato juice *or* orange juice

j) How to ask if a person prefers one particular thing to another

Do you prefer	French food	to	Chinese?
	playing football	or	watching it?

Would you	prefer to / rather	go to the cinema	than	stay at home?
		have tea	or	coffee?

and answer:

Yes,	I do. / I would.	No,	I don't. / I wouldn't.

Well,	to be honest, actually, to tell you the truth,	I really	don't mind. / wouldn't mind.
		I have no preference. I like both (equally well). I don't like either. I wouldn't really like (to do) either.	

k) How to ask how a person would prefer to spend his/her time

What	do you prefer / would you prefer to / would you rather	do(ing) at weekends?
Where		go(ing) for your holidays?
When		get(ting) up in the mornings?
Who		watch(ing)?

Stay(ing) at home	or	go(ing) out somewhere?
Spain		somewhere in Britain?
Early		late?
Leeds		Manchester United?

...ces, Dislikes and Preferences

Why	do you prefer would you prefer to would you rather	be(ing) single	to than	be(ing) married?

and answer:

I prefer		go(ing) out somewhere. go(ing) to Spain.
I'd	prefer to rather	get(ting) up late. watch(ing) Arsenal. be(ing) single because you've got more friends.

l) How to ask about types of preferences

What	sort of kind of type of	books	do you prefer		read(ing)?
		music	would you	prefer to rather	listen(ing) to?
		food			eat(ing)?

Science fiction		detective stories?
Classical music	or	pop music?
French food		Italian food?

and answer:

I prefer		read(ing) science fiction. listen(ing) to pop music. eat(ing) Italian food.
I'd	prefer to rather	

Unit 5: Likes, Dislikes and Preferences

PRACTICE 7

Work in pairs. Take turns to ask and answer questions about your preferences, using the ideas below and changing the verb where necessary. Ask and answer in as many different ways as possible.

1. Rolls-Royces or Volvos?
2. travel by bus or by train?
3. coffee or tea?
4. go to the theatre or to the cinema?
5. what to wear – jumpers or T-shirts?
6. where to go for your holidays – Sweden or Greece?
7. when to visit Spain – July or September?
8. what sort of people to be with – people from your own country or foreigners?
9. what kind of car to drive – sports cars or saloon cars?
10. what type of job to have – a well-paid one or an interesting one?

Written Practice 2

Complete the following dialogues:

1. A: I much prefer .... to ....
   B: .... (*agrees*)

2. A: I'd prefer to .... than ....
   B: .... (*disagrees*)

3. A: I'd rather .... than ....
   B: .... (*says he/she doesn't know*)

4. A: Do you prefer .... to ....?
   B: ....
   A: .... (*agrees*)

5. A: Would you rather .... than ....?
   B: ....
   A: .... (*disagrees*)

6. A: Would you prefer to .... than ....?
   B: ....
   A: .... (*says he/she doesn't mind*)

7. A: I like ....
   B: .... (*agrees*) But I prefer ....
   A: .... (*disagrees*)

Unit 5: Likes, Dislikes and Preferences

Dialogue

Practise reading the following dialogue in pairs. Read the dialogue again, replacing the phrases in **bold** with phrases of similar meaning. Then write out the new dialogue.

A: Guess what? They're showing 'China Seas' with Clark Gable on TV tonight.

B: Are they really? Oh, I must watch that! If there's one actor I **love** watching it's Clark Gable.

A: Yes, **so do I,** especially when he's playing opposite Jean Harlow.

B: Jean Harlow? Oh, I **can't stand her!**

A: **Can't you?** But why not?

B: I don't know. I just **don't like** the way she acts, that's all.

A: But she was a very good actress!

B: You must be joking!

A: No I'm not. I really **like** the way she acts. Anyway, **I'd much rather** watch 'China Seas' than the opera on B.B.C. 2, 'La Traviata'.

B: You're not serious, are you? You really mean to say that **you'd prefer to** watch 'China Seas'?

A: Yes. Any day.

B: Well... if that's the **sort of** film you **enjoy** watching, then all I can say is that I don't think very much of your taste! I shall watch the opera!

Unit 5: Likes, Dislikes and Preferences

Role-Play

CHOOSING A HOLIDAY

Work in groups of three.

Before starting, read through the following and tick the answer you agree with most.

A

	I love	I like	I quite like	I don't like	I hate	I can't stand
going abroad.						
travelling by air.						
travelling by boat.						
lying on the beach all day.						
lots of sun.						
meeting the local people.						
going to night clubs and discotheques.						
visiting museums and art galleries.						
eating foreign food.						

B Tick which you prefer:

	a place with lots of people	a place with not many people	
	staying at a hotel	camping	
	places where they speak English	places where they do not speak English	
	somewhere modern	somewhere old-fashioned	
	spending a lot of money	not spending a lot of money	
	travelling with a lot of people	travelling with a few people	
	a summer holiday	a winter holiday	
	being in a town	being in the country	
	a lot of sunshine	not too much sunshine	
	staying in one place	visiting lots of places	

Unit 5: Likes, Dislikes and Preferences

Each group has decided to go on holiday together in Scotland and is trying to choose a suitable holiday from the choices below.

Each person talks about his likes, dislikes and preferences, etc., and the group eventually chooses one of the holidays.

INCLUSIVE SKI HOLIDAYS
aviemore CENTRE
chalets motel

7th January to 3rd February, 1978 22nd April to 19th May, 1978	4th February to 23rd March, 1978 8th to 21st April 1978
5 Days	
£51·75	£57·50
7 Days	
£66·00 (PLUS VAT)	£73·50

For further details and bookings contact:-
Harry Abrahams, Chalets Manager,
Aviemore Centre, Inverness-shire
Tel:- (0479) 810618

Scottish Highland Hotels...

the perfect choice for your Scottish holiday — with 15 hotels throughout Scotland's most scenic areas. Write for touring guide, tariff including special Spring and Autumn rates
to: — **Central Reservations, Scottish Highland Hotels, 98 West George Street, Glasgow, G2 1PW.**
Tel: 041-332 6538.

SELF-CATERING HOLIDAYS

Taynuilt 1 mile, Oban 12 miles. A country house standing in its own grounds amidst magnificent mountain scenery, divided into 8 flats, well equipped and furnished, to sleep 2, 4, or 6 people. Write for a brochure with s.a.e. and quote "SJG" to
LONAN HOUSE,
TAYNUILT, ARGYLL.
Tel: 086 62 253.

St. Andrews
THE HOME OF GOLF.

A Royal and Ancient town with an appeal to every one. Lots to do and see plus four first class golf courses.
Where to stay and information leaflets available free from:
**Information Centre
Room 2
South Street
St Andrews
Fife KY16 9JX**

Caravans For Hire

On one of Scotland's best parks. Magnificent views, fishing, boating, sailing. Ideal centre for touring the Highlands.

S.A.E. for brochure to:-

**Dept. T
LINNHE CARAVAN PARK
CORPACH   FORT WILLIAM**

EDINBURGH

The city that gives you a Military Tattoo, an International Festival, a Magnificent Castle, Museums, Art Galleries, Fine Restaurants, Excellent Hotels and a warm welcome. For information on accommodation and things to do and see send 15p stamp to:
**Room E
The City of Edinburgh District Council
1 Cockburn Street, Edinburgh EH1 1BR**
A Golden Rail Resort

The Freedom Inn

offers the unique option of self-catering or full hotel facilities allowing you to have a family holiday in a luxury hotel at a price you can afford.

**Freedom Inn.
Aviemore Centre.
Aviemore, Inverness-shire PH22 1PF
0479 810 781**

AYR PRESTWICK TROON GIRVAN

KYLE & CARRICK DISTRICT

Scotland's holiday corner

Ayr, Prestwick, Troon and Girvan — the land of Burns — a place of sea, sun and glorious sands. Sailing, fishing, golf and entertainments for the whole family. Send crossed 25p P.O for our full colour brochure to Tourist Information Centres at
30 Miller Rd., Ayr & Bridge St., Girvan

Blakes Holidays

Boating holidays.
Luxury hire cruisers and yachts on Loch Ness and the Caledonian Canal or the West Coast. Fully equipped for holiday comfort.

Holiday Cottages and Chalets in the Highlands and Islands. Specially selected, ideal for fishing, golfing, riding, boating etc.

Tel: 06053 3226 Or write Blakes Holidays, (Dept. ST), Wroxham, Norwich NR12 8DH.

Group Work: Talking about Likes, Dislikes and Preferences

Read through the following sentences, then tick (√) the answer you agree with most. When you have finished, compare your answers with someone else in the class. (Try to give reasons for your likes, dislikes or preferences.)

	I agree	I disagree	I'm not sure
1. I hate going to the dentist.			
2. Most men prefer blondes to brunettes.			
3. I hate being alone for more than a few hours.			
4. Most young people prefer pop music to classical music.			
5. I love meeting new people.			
6. I can't stand people who snore.			
7. I don't like staying in at weekends.			
8. I prefer female teachers to male teachers.			
9. Most women would rather go out to work when they are married than stay at home to look after the children.			
10. There are very few jobs in the home (e.g. ironing, making the beds) I like doing.			
11. I don't like getting up in the mornings.			
12. Most parents would prefer their son or daughter to marry someone of their own nationality, colour and religion.			
13. I'm not very keen on my Christian name.			
14. Most people would like to be millionaires.			
15. I really like learning English.			
16. Most people would like to get married before they are twenty-five.			

Unit 6:
Invitations

It is Tuesday evening. Joanna has just come home from work when the phone rings.

JOANNA: Hello, 5621.
SIMON: Hello, Jo. It's me – Simon. Do you remember – from the party?
JOANNA: Oh, yes, of course. Hello, Simon.
SIMON: Listen, Jo, I was wondering if you were doing anything on Saturday afternoon?
JOANNA: Er ... Saturday?
SIMON: Only, if not, would you like to come to Stratford for the day? They say *The Merchant of Venice* is really marvellous!
JOANNA: Yes, I'd love to, but wait a minute – I'll just check in my diary. *[She looks through her diary.]* Hello?
SIMON: Yes?
JOANNA: I'm awfully sorry, Simon, but my mother's coming down from Edinburgh and I've promised to go shopping with her on Saturday afternoon.
SIMON: Oh, that's a pity! But can't you go shopping another day?
JOANNA: No, I'm afraid not. My mother's only staying for a few days.
SIMON: But do you really have to go with her? Can't she go on her own?
JOANNA: Well, she's buying a coat and wants me to go along and help her choose it. I'll have to go with her. She's been looking forward to it for weeks.
SIMON: Ah well, another time perhaps?
JOANNA: Yes, fine. Look, why not the weekend after next? It's still on then, isn't it?
SIMON: Yes, I think so. A week on Saturday, then. I'll pick you up at about 2 o'clock. O.K.?
JOANNA: Yes, lovely. Thank you. I look forward to it.

The Shakespeare Memorial Theatre at Stratford

Unit 6: Invitations

a) How to invite others to do something (with you)

When you invite someone to do something with you, here are some phrases you can use:

Would you like to I was wondering if you'd care to How would you like to Do you want to	come to a party with me on Friday?
I was wondering if you felt like How do you fancy How about Do you feel like	coming to Brighton with me tomorrow afternoon?

b) How to accept an invitation

Yes,	I'd love to. I'd like to very much. I'd like that very much. that sounds (nice/lovely/super). that sounds like a good idea. that would be (very) nice.	Thank you (very much).

PRACTICE 1

Practise inviting someone to do something with you using the following words:

1. having dinner with me tonight?
2. coming round to my place tonight?
3. have dinner with me some time next week?

63

Unit 6: Invitations

4. spend the weekend with me in the South of France?
5. come to the pictures tonight?
6. visiting the new art gallery on Saturday?
7. going to the theatre with me tomorrow?
8. see *Hamlet* next Thursday?

c) How to turn down an invitation politely

I'd really like to It's nice of you to ask I'd love to	but	I just can't, I'm afraid. I (really) don't think I can. honestly, I really can't.
I won't be able to, I'm afraid,		thanks all the same.

Unit 6: Invitations

PRACTICE 2

Work in pairs. A invites B to do something, using the pictures below. B accepts or refuses the invitation politely. Try to ask and answer in as many different ways as possible.

e.g.

> A: *Would you like to* come out with me tonight?
> B: *Yes, I'd love to.* Thank you very much.
>   or
> B: *I'd really like to, but I can't, I'm afraid.*

Unit 6: Invitations

d) How to accept an invitation and ask for further details

Yes, (I'd love to) but	where exactly? what time? when exactly? which day?

PRACTICE 3

Work in pairs. A invites B to do something, using the words below. B accepts the invitation and asks for further details, using the word in brackets.

e.g.

> A: *How about* meeting me after work tomorrow?
> B: *Yes, I'd love to*, but *what time exactly?*
> A: *About 5.30?*
> B: Yes, fine. See you *tomorrow*, then.

1. come to my party (*day?*)
2. see the film at the Plaza with me tomorrow evening (*time?*)
3. come to the football match on Saturday (*match?*)
4. help me move into my new flat (*when?*)
5. come for a drive in my car tomorrow (*where?*)
6. have lunch with me tomorrow (*time?*)

e) How to turn down an invitation but suggest an alternative time or day

Oh dear, I can't (on Friday). I'm afraid I'm busy then. I'm sorry but I can't (tomorrow). I'm afraid (Friday's) a bit difficult. No, (tomorrow's) impossible, I'm afraid. Unfortunately, I can't on (Friday).	But another time perhaps? Can't you make it another day/time? Isn't there any other day/time that would suit you? What about another (night)? But I'm free on (Tuesday). Couldn't we meet then?

PRACTICE 4

Work in pairs. A invites B to do something, using the words below. B turns down the invitation but tries to arrange an alternative day or time. Ask and answer in as many different ways as possible.

e.g.

> A: *How would you like to* come fishing with me on Wednesday?
> B: *Oh dear, I can't on Wednesday. Can't you make it another day?*
> A: What about *Thursday*, then?
> B: Yes, *Thursday's* fine. Thank you very much.

1. come to the theatre with me tomorrow night
2. see my parents on Saturday
3. come to my flat for a meal tonight
4. meet me at Victoria station at 6.30
5. go to the dance with me on Friday
6. have dinner with me on Monday evening

f) How to turn down an invitation with an excuse

When you want to make an excuse, here are some phrases you can use:

I'm awfully sorry but	I've got to go somewhere on Friday.
I'm sorry but I can't.	I really must do some work tonight.
Oh dear! I'm afraid I can't.	I have to visit my mother on Friday.
I hope you don't mind but	I really can't afford the time.
I can't, I'm afraid.	I've already arranged to go somewhere.
	I just don't feel up to it tonight.
	I'm really much too busy at the moment.

PRACTICE 5

Work in pairs. A invites B to do something, using the pictures shown. B turns down the invitation with an excuse.

e.g.

> A: *Do you feel like* coming to the pub with me tonight?
> B: *Oh dear! I'm afraid I can't. I've already arranged to go somewhere tonight.*
> A: Ah well. Another time, perhaps?
> B: Yes, fine.

Unit 6: Invitations

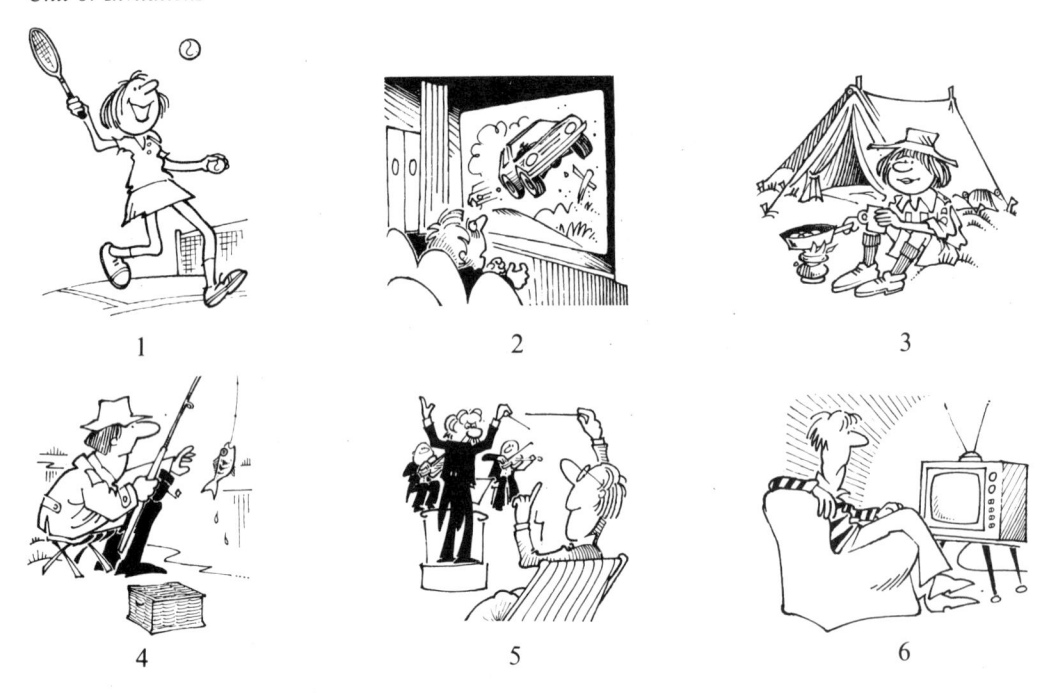

1   2   3
4   5   6

g) How to persist with an invitation to try to persuade others to change their minds

If a person turns down your invitation, you can always persist and try to make him change his mind. Here are some phrases you can use:

Oh, come on.	It should be fun/interesting.
Are you (quite) sure you can't?	I promise it'll be fun/worth it.
Oh, surely you can!	Just for me, eh?
Are you absolutely sure?	I'd really appreciate it.

h) How to give in to persuasion

Oh,	all right (then), very well, as you wish,	just for you. but it had better be (good). but I shouldn't really.
Well,	perhaps I can (after all), if you really want me to, if you're sure it'll be (fun),	just this once. you know I can't refuse you anything. but I mustn't be home too late.

PRACTICE 6

Work in pairs. A invites B to do something, using the words below. B turns down the invitation politely at first. Then after A persists, B gives in.

e.g.

> A: *Would you like to come with me to the cinema tonight?*
> B: *I'd love to, but honestly, I can't.*
> A: *Oh, come on. Just for me, eh?*
> B: *Oh, very well. Just for you.*

1. play golf
2. go to a football match
3. go to a concert
4. go to John's party
5. come over to watch a programme on TV
6. come for tea

i) How to resist persuasion politely

No,	honestly, I mean it, I'm afraid (I'm) sorry,	I really can't.	But thanks all the same.
	I've really got to (do some work). I really must refuse. I really can't. it's really impossible.		
	it's very kind of you, but I don't think		I'd better. I will.

Unit 6: Invitations

PRACTICE 7

Work in pairs. A invites B to do something, using the following:

1. meet me after work today
2. go to London with me on Boxing Day
3. join us for bridge on Friday
4. come round for a meal on Christmas Eve
5. hitch-hike to Dover on Sunday
6. watch me play football on Saturday afternoon

B, using the diary below, politely turns down the invitation and refuses to give in to persuasion.

> A: *How would you like to* come to a party tonight?
> B: *I can't, I'm afraid. I have to revise for my English exam.*
> A: *Oh, come on. I'd really appreciate it.*
> B: *No, I'm sorry, I really must revise for this exam.* But thanks all the same.

DECEMBER	DECEMBER
23 Monday dentist 5.30pm	27 Friday party 8.30pm
24 Tuesday Office party	28 Saturday hairdresser 3.45
25 Wednesday spend the day with mum and dad	29 Sunday revise for English exam.
26 Thursday Brighton for the day	

Unit 6: Invitations

Written Practice

Complete the following dialogues according to the instructions in brackets.

1. A: .... come riding with me at the weekend?
   B: .... (*accepts*)

2. A: I was wondering if you'd care to ....
   B: .... (*politely refuses*)

3. A: .... going for a drive tomorrow?
   B: .... (*accepts but asks for further details*)
   A: .... (*gives details*)
   B: ....

4. A: I was wondering if you felt like .... tomorrow night?
   B: .... (*turns it down but tries to arrange another night*)
   A: ....? (*suggests another night*)
   B: .... (*accepts*)

5. A: .... go for a drink with me tonight?
   B: ....   (*turns it down with an excuse*)
   A: Ah well, ..., perhaps?
   B: ....

6. A: How do you fancy ....?
   B: .... (*politely refuses*)
   A: .... (*persists*)
   B: .... (*gives in*)

7. A: .... coming in for a quick drink?
   B: .... (*refuses with an excuse*)
   A: .... (*persists*)
   B: .... (*refuses to give in*)

8. A: Would you like to .... some time next week?
   B: .... (*accepts but asks for further details*)
   A: .... (*gives details*)
   B: ....

Unit 6: Invitations

Dialogue

Practise reading the following dialogue in pairs. Read the dialogue again, replacing the phrases in **bold** with phrases of similar meaning. Then write out the new dialogue.

A: Hello. **Claire Brown** speaking.

B: Hello, **Claire**. It's me – **Brian**.

A: Oh, hello, **Brian**.

B: Listen. **Would you like to** come to the Tate with me?

A: Er ... when exactly?

B: On **Friday afternoon**.

A: **Oh, I'm awfully sorry, Brian,** but I've got to see someone on **Friday**.

B: **Oh, come on. I promise it'll be fun.**

A: **No, honestly, I really can't.**

B: **Oh, surely you can? Just for me, eh?**

A: **No, I'm sorry, Brian.** I've really got to see someone. But another day, perhaps?

B: Well ... what about **Sunday,** then?

A: Yes, **Sunday's** fine.

B: Oh, good! I'll pick you up at **3.30**. O.K.?

A: Yes, all right. Thank you very much. 'Bye.

B: 'Bye. See you on **Sunday**.

The Tate Gallery

Role-Play

SITUATION 1: ARRANGING A BUSINESS MEETING

Work in pairs. You are two businessmen/businesswomen who are trying to arrange a meeting. Before starting, look at the diaries on page 183 (Person A) and page 188 (Person B).

SITUATION 2: INVITING SOMEONE TO DINNER

Work in pairs. Person A reads through the notes below, while Person B reads through the notes on page 188. Do this now!

Person A. You phone up Person B to invite him/her to dinner at your flat one evening next week. You are free every evening, so you are prepared to choose an evening which suits Person B best.

Unit 7: Requests and Offers

Joanna is having a flat-warming party tonight and is getting ready for it. Simon has come round to her flat to help her.

JOANNA: Oh, Simon, do you think you could help me move the table, please?
SIMON: Yes, of course. Where do you want it?
JOANNA: Er ... over there by the wall, I think. It'll give us a bit more room for dancing, won't it?
SIMON: Yes, good idea.
  [They move the table.]
JOANNA: Thanks. Now ... what else?
SIMON: Shall I move the sofa too?
JOANNA: No, there's no need, thanks. It can stay where it is. But you could take those chairs to the bedroom, I suppose. We don't really need them in here.
SIMON: Yes, O.K.
JOANNA: Oh, thanks. And while you're doing that I can go and see if the chicken's ready.
  [Simon takes the chairs into the bedroom. Joanna goes into the kitchen and opens the oven door.]
SIMON: Hey, Joanna! The light's gone.
JOANNA: Sorry, I can't hear you.
  [Simon leaves the bedroom and enters the kitchen. Joanna is getting the chicken out of the oven. It looks heavy.]
SIMON: Here, let me give you a hand with that.
JOANNA: No – don't touch! It's hot. *[She puts it down near the sink.]* There! Now, what did you say?
SIMON: I said the light's gone in the bedroom.
JOANNA: Oh, it hasn't, has it? That's a nuisance! I haven't got any spare bulbs anywhere.
SIMON: Well, would you like me to pop out and buy one? The shop on the corner's still open. It won't take me a minute.
JOANNA: Oh, would you, Simon? I'd be ever so grateful.
SIMON: Yes, of course. And then when I come back I can fix up the speakers for the music.

a) How to make a request

When you ask someone to do something, here are some polite phrases you can use:

Would / Could / Will	you	(give me a lift home tonight), please?
I wonder if	you'd / you could	
Would you mind		(giving me a lift home)?

b) How to respond favourably to a request

Yes,	of course. / certainly.
No,	not at all. / of course not.

PRACTICE 1

Work in pairs. Take turns to make and agree to a request, using the words below. Try to ask and answer in as many different ways as possible.

1. help me to move into my new house
2. open the window
3. take the car to the garage
4. put the lights off when you go to bed
5. tell John I can't see him tomorrow
6. lend me your rubber
7. see who's at the door
8. take these letters to the post office

c) How to refuse a request politely

I'm sorry, I can't. / Sorry, I can't, I'm afraid. / I'm afraid I can't because / I'm terribly sorry but	(I have to rush off to my sister's after the lesson).

Unit 7: Requests and Offers

PRACTICE 2

Work in pairs. A makes polite requests, using the words below. B refuses politely, using the words in brackets. Try to ask and answer in as many different ways as possible.

1. give me a lift to the party (*I'm not taking the car.*)
2. post this letter (*I'm not going anywhere near the post office.*)
3. baby-sit for me on Thursday (*I've got to go to a meeting.*)
4. help me with my homework (*It's too difficult for me, too.*)
5. pick me up from the theatre (*The car's still at the garage.*)
6. work overtime tonight (*I've promised my mother I'd take her to the theatre.*)
7. lend me £2 (*I've only got 50p on me.*)
8. help me move the piano (*My doctor's told me I mustn't lift heavy weights.*)

d) How to ask permission to do something

When you ask someone for permission to do something, here are some polite phrases you can use:

May / Can / Could	I		(go home early tonight)?
Do you think / I wonder if	I could		
Is it all right if I			
Do you mind if I			(smoke)?

e) How to grant permission

Yes,	certainly.
	of course.
	of course you (may/can/could).
	all right.
	that's (quite) all right (by me).
	by all means.
	please do.
	go ahead.
No,	of course not.
	not at all.

Unit 7: Requests and Offers

f) How to refuse permission politely

No, I'm afraid you can't.
I'm sorry, but you can't.
Well, I'd rather you didn't, if you don't mind.

Yes, I'm afraid I do.
I'm sorry, but I do.
Well, I'd rather you didn't, if you don't mind.

PRACTICE 3

Work in pairs. Take turns to ask for and grant permission using the pictures and words given. Try to ask and answer in as many different ways as possible.

1. smoke
2. open the window 
3. use the phone 
4. come in 
5. take off my tie 
6. switch on the television

Unit 7: Requests and Offers

7. play the piano

8. take my shoes off

PRACTICE 4

Look at the pictures in Practice 3 again. This time, take turns to ask for and politely refuse permission. Try to ask and answer in as many different ways as possible.

g) How to refuse permission strongly

Certainly not!
No, you (most certainly) can't!
No, I'm afraid that's quite out of the question.
No, it's (just) not allowed.
Over my dead body!

Yes,	I most certainly do!
	I'm afraid I do.
	I do.
	most strongly!

PRACTICE 5

Now take turns to ask for and strongly refuse permission, using the words below. Again, try to ask and answer in as many different ways as possible.

1. marry your daughter
2. borrow your car for the summer
3. play the bagpipes
4. stay the night
5. invite mother for the weekend
6. put your name down as the next Conservative candidate
7. borrow your flat for the weekend
8. have next week off to go fishing

Written Practice 1

Complete the following dialogues. In each one politely refuse the request and give a reason for your refusal.

1. A: .... take my mother to the hospital on Friday, please?
   B: ....

2. A: .... baby-sit for me tonight?
   B: ....

3. A: .... post this letter for me, please?
   B: ....

4. A: .... help me with my homework?
   B: ....

5. A: .... work overtime on Tuesday?
   B: ....

6. A: .... meeting John at the station?
   B: ....

h) How to offer to do something

When you offer to do something, here are some polite phrases you can use:

Shall I	
Would you like me to	(help you move into your new flat)?
Do you want me to	

i) How to accept the offer

Yes, please.	Thank you.
That's very kind of you.	Thanks a lot.
Oh, you wouldn't, would you?	Thank you very much.
Oh, that would be marvellous!	Thanks awfully.
Oh, would you really?	Thanks a million.

Unit 7: Requests and Offers

PRACTICE 6

Work in pairs. Take turns to make and accept offers, using the pictures and words below. Try to ask and answer in as many different ways as possible.

1. type the letters
2. help you with that luggage 
3. post the letters 
4. give you a lift 
5. get you an aspirin 
6. help you move house 
7. play some records 
8. push the car

j) How to refuse the offer politely

> No, thank you/thanks. I can manage.
> No, there's no need. But thank you/thanks all the same.
> No, that's all right, thank you.
> Well, that's very kind of you, but I think I can manage, thanks.

PRACTICE 7

Look at the pictures in Practice 6 again, and take turns to make and politely refuse offers. Try to ask and answer in as many different ways as possible.

k) How to give warnings

When you want to warn people not to do something or to take care, here are some phrases you can use:

Don't	move! touch! It's hot. sit on that chair. It's broken! say that to him. He's sensitive about his family.	
Mind	out! the step! your head! the dog!	Watch out! Look out! Be careful! Take care!

PRACTICE 8

Practise giving warnings, using the following drawings. In each case write down the words you think the person is saying.

1   2   3

Unit 7: Requests and Offers

4   5   6

Written Practice 2

Write down suitable offers in reply to the following and accept or politely refuse the offer.

1. A: Oh dear! My library book's overdue and I'm going to London today.
   B: . . . .
   A: . . . .

2. A: Oh, John! I've left my money at home!
   B: . . . .
   A: . . . .

3. A: Oh, no! I've just missed the last bus!
   B: . . . .
   A: . . . .

4. A: I'm moving into my new flat on Saturday.
   B: . . . .
   A: . . . .

5. A: I've got an awful headache.
   B: . . . .
   A: . . . .

6. A: It's so hot in here!
   B: . . . .
   A: . . . .

Dialogue

Practise reading the following dialogue in pairs. Read the dialogue again, replacing the phrases in **bold** with phrases of similar meaning. Then write out the new dialogue.

A: Oh, Miss Brown, **would you** post this letter, please?

B: Yes, **certainly**. And **shall I** take this parcel to the post office, too?

A: Yes, please. Oh, and Miss Brown ...

B: Yes?

A: **Could you** work overtime on Friday?

B: **I'm terribly sorry, but** I've already made arrangements to go somewhere on Friday.

A: Oh, I see.
   [pause]

B: **May I** go now?

A: What? Oh, yes ... **yes, of course.**

Role-Play

ARRANGING A PARTY

Work in groups of five students – A, B, C, D and E. You have decided to have an end-of-term party and are meeting to work out the necessary arrangements. Here are some of the things that will have to be worked out:

1. whose flat the party will be held at.
2. who will help to get it ready (move furniture, clean it, tidy up etc.).
3. how many people to invite. Only people in the class or boyfriends, girlfriends, other students etc.?
4. what time the party will start and finish.
5. how much food is needed. What sort? Who will buy/make it?
6. what sort of music to have. Who can bring records?
7. other items that need to be brought – knives, forks, plates, glasses etc. Who can bring what?
8. who will help tidy up after the party – move back furniture, wash up etc.
9. anything else you can think of.

Before you start, read through your role on page 180.

Unit 8:
Opinions

Brian, Claire and Peter are students. Sally and Peter have invited Brian and Claire to dinner.

SALLY: Brian, you've seen *Star Wars*, haven't you?
BRIAN: Yes, that's right.
SALLY: What did you think of it?
BRIAN: Well, I was a bit disappointed, really. I didn't think it was a particularly good film at all.
CLAIRE: Oh, I disagree, Brian! I thought it was great! It's one of the best films I've seen. Don't you think so, Peter?
PETER: Yes, I agree up to a point. It was good ... I enjoyed it ... but, to be honest, it wasn't as good as I thought it would be...
BRIAN: That's exactly how I felt. If you ask me, it was just one big publicity stunt from start to finish.
CLAIRE: Oh, that's rubbish, Brian! You're the first person I've met who hasn't enjoyed the film.
BRIAN: Perhaps I am ... but Sally asked me for my opinion, and as far as I'm concerned it was pretty boring.
PETER: Ah ... I'm not so sure I'd agree with you there, Brian. I don't see how you can say it was boring.
CLAIRE: Neither do I. It was full of excitement! All the way through!

BRIAN: In my opinion it wasn't. I was bored ... mainly because I was expecting so much more to happen, I suppose.
CLAIRE: Oh, come on! A lot happened!
PETER: I agree with you, Brian, about expecting a lot more to happen. So did I.
CLAIRE: Oh, you're both talking nonsense! Don't listen to them, Sally. Believe me, it's really exciting – you'll love every minute of it. In fact, why don't you and I go and see it tomorrow?
SALLY: But you've already seen it!
CLAIRE: So what? This is one film I'd gladly see again. And enjoy it just as much, too!

Unit 8: Opinions

a) How to ask for an opinion

When you ask someone for their opinion about something, here are some phrases you can use:

What do you think of/about What's your opinion of How do you find How do you feel about	British television?

b) How to give an opinion

I think (that) In my opinion, If you ask me, As I see it, As far as I'm concerned, If you want my opinion, (Speaking) personally, I think My view is that The way I look at it is this –	there are some very good programmes. there is too much violence on the screen today. television is a bad influence.

PRACTICE 1

Work in pairs, taking turns to ask for and to give opinions about the subjects below. Try to use as many different sentence-openings as you can.

1. the women's liberation movement

2. American films

3. 'spaghetti' Westerns

Unit 8: Opinions

4. the 'Miss World' contest

5. Wimbledon

6. hi-jackers

7. rock and roll

8. the Eurovision song contest

c) How to agree strongly with an opinion

Yes,	so do I.
	I (quite) agree.
	I entirely agree with you.
	they certainly should.
	they should, shouldn't they?
	you're quite right.
	that's just how I see it.
	that's exactly my opinion.
	that's how I feel.
	exactly!

PRACTICE 2

Work in pairs. Go through the pictures in Practice 1 again, taking turns to give and to agree strongly with an opinion. Try to use as many different phrases as possible.

d) How to half-agree with an opinion

Opinion: I think smoking should be banned.

Well, yes, Yes, I agree, Yes, perhaps, Yes, in a way, Mmm, possibly, Yes, I agree up to a point, Yes, I suppose so, Yes, I dare say you're right,	but (it would be a very difficult thing to do).

PRACTICE 3

Work in pairs. Take it in turns to give and to half-agree with an opinion, using the words below. Try to use as many different phrases as possible.

1. Women are (as intelligent as/less intelligent than/more intelligent than) men.
2. American films are (terrific/awful/the best in the world).
3. Rock and roll is (dead/alive/more alive than ever).
4. Television is the (greatest/worst) invention of the twentieth century.
5. Elizabeth Taylor (is/is not) the most attractive woman in the world.

e) How to disagree politely with an opinion

I'm not so sure (really).
Do you think so?
Well, it depends.
I'm not so certain.
Well, I don't know.
Well, I'm not so sure about that.
Mmm, I'm not really sure you're right.
No, I don't think so really.

f) How to disagree strongly with an opinion

No,	I disagree. I disagree with you entirely. I'm afraid I don't agree. I don't agree with you (at all). I'm afraid you're wrong there. I really can't agree. I wouldn't accept that for one minute. I don't think they should.

PRACTICE 4

Work in pairs. Take it in turns to give and to disagree politely or strongly with an opinion, using the words below. Try to use as many different phrases as possible.

1. Hunting (should/should not) be banned.
2. English is a very (difficult/easy) language to learn.
3. There's too (much/little) discussion about women's rights today.
4. We need (more/fewer) nuclear power stations.
5. Taxes are (too high/not high enough).
6. Parents (should/should not) have to pay for their children's education.

g) How to disagree strongly and impolitely with an opinion

Opinion: I think smoking should be banned.

Oh! Come on! That's rubbish! You must be joking! What nonsense! Never! You can't be serious! You're not serious – surely! You can't really mean that!	(Just because you don't smoke!)

PRACTICE 5

Work in pairs. Go through the opinions in Practice 4 again, taking turns to give and to disagree strongly and impolitely with an opinion.

Written Practice

Complete the following dialogues:

1. A: .... it's better to be single than married.
   B: .... (*agrees*)

2. A: .... nuclear power is our only hope for the future.
   B: .... (*disagrees*)

3. A: ...., everyone has a perfect right to smoke whenever and wherever they like.
   B: .... (*disagrees strongly and impolitely*)

4. A: .... people who drink and drive?
   B: ...., anyone who drinks and drives is irresponsible.
   A: .... (*agrees*)

5. A: .... learning English?
   B: ...., English is a very difficult language to learn.
   A: .... (*half-agrees*)

6. A: .... television?
   B: ...., television kills conversation.
   A: .... (*disagrees politely*)

Dialogue

Practise reading the following dialogue in groups of three. Read the dialogue again, replacing the phrases in **bold** with phrases of similar meaning. Then write out the new dialogue.

A: **What do you think of** drinking and driving?

B: Well, **in my opinion,** people who drive shouldn't drink.

A: Yes, **I quite agree.**

C: **I'm not so sure really.** I think they should be allowed to drink a little.

B: **No, I'm afraid I don't agree.** Once people start drinking, they never know when to stop.

A: **Yes, I agree, but** maybe it's asking too much to ban it altogether. And what about all the pubs in the country? You can't get to them without a car!

B: Well, **as I see it,** the obvious answer is to close them all down.

C: **That's nonsense!** There are thousands of country pubs in Britain. No one would agree to closing them down.

B: **Mmm, possibly,** but it's about time we took drinking and driving a little more seriously.

A: Yes, **I entirely agree with you.**

Pair Work: Opinions and Attitudes

Questionnaire – work and jobs

Read through the sentences below, then put a circle around the number which most closely coincides with your opinion. Before starting, look at the Key. When you have finished, discuss your answers with someone else in the class. Give reasons for your opinion – and argue with your partner if you don't agree with him/her.

Key
1 = I agree completely
2 = I agree on the whole
3 = I can't make up my mind
4 = I disagree on the whole
5 = I disagree completely

1. Pop singers, film-stars and sportsmen earn far too much money.	1 2 3 4 5
2. Housewives should be paid a salary for looking after a home and a family.	1 2 3 4 5
3. There are certain jobs that are not really suitable for women.	1 2 3 4 5
4. The computer will be the main reason for unemployment in the future.	1 2 3 4 5
5. The most important thing about a job is the money.	1 2 3 4 5
6. Most people are not really happy with their present jobs.	1 2 3 4 5
7. If I won a lot of money I would stop working.	1 2 3 4 5
8. A job is more important to most people than their free time.	1 2 3 4 5
9. Strikes are nearly always a bad thing. (Nobody really wins.)	1 2 3 4 5
10. It is better to have any sort of job than no job at all.	1 2 3 4 5
11. Most people in the future will have at least three entirely different sorts of jobs.	1 2 3 4 5
12. Unemployment amongst young people could be reduced if the Government forced people to retire when they were 55 instead of 65.	1 2 3 4 5

Unit 9: Problems and Advice

At college, Peter has noticed that Brian seems worried about something. He decides to ask him what the problem is.

PETER: You look a bit worried, Brian. Is anything wrong?

BRIAN: No, not really.

PETER: Are you sure? You don't seem yourself today, somehow.

BRIAN: Well... I've got to find a new flat somewhere. They're going to pull down the building where I'm living at the moment.

PETER: Well, is that such a problem?

BRIAN: Yes, it is – when you've only got a week to do it in.

PETER: A week? That seems rather short notice.

BRIAN: Oh, I've known about it for ages, but I haven't done anything about it until now. I kept meaning to, but never got round to it somehow.

PETER: Oh, I see. Well, Brian, if I were you I'd start looking through the papers straight away.

BRIAN: I have... every day for the last week.

PETER: And you haven't found anywhere?

BRIAN: No, not a thing. The flats were either too expensive or too far away, or someone had already beaten me to it. So I really don't know what to do.

PETER: Hmm. I see your problem. But perhaps you could put an advert in the paper – you know – saying you're looking for a flat.

BRIAN: Yes, I could do that, I suppose, but it all takes time, doesn't it? And if that doesn't work then I'm worse off than before.

PETER: Yes. I can see why you're worried. *[a slight pause]* Hey! Wait a minute! Of course! How stupid of me!

BRIAN: What, Peter?

PETER: Ken – my brother – he's an estate agent. I'm sure he'll be able to help you. Why don't you and I go round and see him after work?

BRIAN: Well, that sounds a marvellous idea, I must say. But are you sure he'll be able to help?

PETER: Yes, of course. I am his brother, remember. So don't worry. He'll find you somewhere – wait and see.

BRIAN: Oh, that's wonderful, Peter. Thanks a lot. That's certainly taken a weight off my mind.

a) How to ask someone about his/her problem

When you ask someone about his/her problem, here are some phrases you can use:

| You look a bit | worried, upset, | (Jane). | What's | the matter? wrong? up? the problem? |
| | | | Is anything | the matter? wrong? bothering you? |

to which the person can answer:

I've got a pain in my back. or *Yes. I've just lost my job.*

PRACTICE 1

Work in pairs. A asks B if he/she has a problem. B answers, using the words below. Try to ask in as many different ways as possible.

1. My mother's been rushed to hospital.
2. I've lost my wallet.
3. I've just been given the sack.
4. I've got a terrible pain in my chest.
5. John's failed his exams.
6. My flat was burgled last night.

b) How to express sympathy

When you hear of a problem, you can respond sympathetically by using one of the following phrases:

Oh,	I'm sorry to hear that. I had no idea. Poor you! you poor thing.	
	what a	pity! shame!
Oh, no! How	dreadful! awful!	

| Oh dear! That's | awful! terrible! a pity! a shame! a bit of bad luck! a blow! |

Unit 9: Problems and Advice

PRACTICE 2

Go through Practice 1 again, this time adding an appropriate expression of sympathy after hearing what the problem is.

c) How to give positive advice

Problem: I've got a pain in my back.

Why don't you If I were you I'd I suggest you I'd advise you to	(go and see a doctor).
I think you should you ought to you'd better	

PRACTICE 3

Match up the problems from A with an appropriate piece of advice from B.

A
My car's been stolen! I forgot to go to the meeting this morning. I've left my purse at home. I've run out of cigarettes. The last train goes in five minutes. I'm in love with Jan. I'm beginning to put on weight.

B
Well,	I think you ought to go and buy some more. if I were you I'd ring up and apologize. I'd advise you to go on a diet. I think you'd better hurry up, then. I suggest you report it to the police immediately. why don't you ask her out, then? I think you should go back and get it.

94

d) How to give tentative advice

Problem: I can't seem to cope any more.

Perhaps Maybe	you ought to / you should	(see a psychiatrist).
Well,	it might be a good idea to / perhaps you could	
Well,	you could consider / you might like to try	(going away somewhere for a short rest).

PRACTICE 4

Take turns to give positive or tentative advice on the following problems:

1. I can't seem to wake up in the mornings.
2. I keep biting my nails.
3. I'm starting to go bald.
4. I don't like my present job.
5. My car won't start in the mornings.
6. I've got terrible toothache.
7. I've lost my passport.
8. I smoke too much.

e) How to accept a piece of advice

Yes,	that sounds a good idea. / I'll do that. / I'm sure that's a good idea. / I'll certainly try that.	Thanks a lot. / Thanks for the advice. / Thank you very much. / Thank you.

Unit 9: Problems and Advice

PRACTICE 5

Work in pairs. A begins by giving advice as shown in the pictures below. B accepts the advice using as many different phrases as possible. A advises B to:

1. see a doctor

2. stop smoking

3. see a psychiatrist

4. sell the house

5. play tennis.

f) How to agree to think about a piece of advice

Well,	that's worth thinking about.	Thank you.
	I'll think about it anyway.	Thanks for the advice.
	I could do that, I suppose.	I can think about it anyway.
	it might be worth trying.	I'll certainly think about it.

PRACTICE 6

Work in pairs. Go through Practice 5 again. This time B agrees to think about the advice.

g) How to refuse a piece of advice politely

I'm not sure, really. Well, to be honest, I've already tried that.		But thanks anyway. But thanks for trying.
Mmm, I doubt if that would	do any good. work.	But thank you all the same.

PRACTICE 7

Work in pairs. A gives advice, using the words below. B refuses the advice politely. A advises B to:

1. go on a course.
2. buy an alarm clock.
3. buy a new car.
4. leave home.
5. eat less.

What do you think the problems were?

Written Practice

Complete the following dialogues:

1. A: ....?
   B: It's .... He doesn't want to see me any more.
   A: .... (*answers sympathetically*)

2. A: ....?
   B: Yes. My son's just bought a set of drums.
   A: .... (*answers sympathetically, then offers tentative advice*)
   B: .... (*accepts advice*)

3. A: I'm so bored these days.
   B: .... (*gives positive advice*)
   A: .... (*accepts*)

4. A: My new car's broken down for the third time.
   B: .... (*gives tentative advice*)
   A: .... (*refuses advice*)

5. A: I never seem to have any money left at the end of the month.
   B: ....
   A: ....

Unit 9: Problems and Advice

Dialogue

Practise reading the following dialogue in pairs. Read the dialogue again, replacing the phrases in **bold** with phrases of similar meaning. Then write out the new dialogue.

A: You look a bit **worried, Claire. What's the matter?**

B: I can't seem to wake up in the mornings.

A: Oh, **dear! That is a problem.** But don't you have an alarm clock?

B: Yes, of course, but I never seem to hear it.

A: Well, **why don't you** buy an electric one? They go on ringing until you switch them off.

B: **Mmm, I doubt if that would do any good.** I'd just switch it off and go back to sleep.

A: Well, **perhaps you could** ask the telephone operator to give you an early morning call. It's not that expensive.

B: **Yes, that sounds a good idea. Thanks a lot.**

A: Not at all. I hope it works.

Role-Play

RADIO PHONE-IN

Work in groups of up to eight students.

Up to four students are a panel of experts on the radio who answer all problems. Four other students are members of the public who phone in for advice.
Before starting, the members of the public look at page 181 (Persons A, B and C) and pages 181–2 (Person D).

Unit 10:
Certainty and Uncertainty

Peter, Claire and Brian have just finished the last paper of their final examinations.

CLAIRE: Well, Brian, do you think you've passed?
BRIAN: No, definitely not. I thought the paper was terrible. I haven't got a hope of getting through.
CLAIRE: But are you sure?
BRIAN: Absolutely. Not a hope!
PETER: Oh, you're always saying that, Brian, but you still manage to come top in all the tests we have, don't you?
BRIAN: Yes, but this time it's different.
PETER: Oh, I doubt that. Believe me, there's very little chance of you failing. Don't you agree, Claire?
CLAIRE: Well, I wouldn't like to say really, Peter. It's always possible to fail, I suppose. And Brian does seem pretty positive.
BRIAN: Yes, and shall I tell you why? For the simple reason that I didn't even finish the paper. I left out the last question completely.
PETER: But that doesn't mean you've definitely failed. They have to take into account your other papers. And you've probably done well in them, haven't you?
BRIAN: Well, I'm almost certain I passed Paper 1 and Paper 2, but I didn't do so well in Paper 4 or the oral.
CLAIRE: Still, if you did well enough in the first two papers then there's a good chance you've passed.
BRIAN: Well, it could happen, I suppose, but I have my doubts. I think I've failed. In fact, I'm sure I have.
PETER: We'll see! I'm still quite sure you've passed. You and Claire.
BRIAN: Well, as you say, we'll see.

Unit 10: Certainty and Uncertainty

a) How to express certainty

When you are sure that something will (or will not) happen in the future, here are some phrases you can use:

e.g. Do you think England will win the next World Cup?

Yes,	I'm	absolutely sure quite sure certain positive	they will.
	of course		

Yes,	definitely. certainly. without doubt. absolutely.		

or

No,	I'm	absolutely sure quite sure certain positive	they won't.
	of course		

No,	definitely certainly absolutely	not.	

PRACTICE 1

Work in pairs. Take turns to ask and answer the following questions, expressing certainty that the event will or will not happen.

Do you think (that):

1. there will be another oil crisis before 1990?
2. Luxemburg will win the next World Cup?
3. a completely 'safe' cigarette will soon be discovered?
4. a cure will ever be found for cancer?

b) How to express probability

When you are almost certain that something will (or will not) happen in the future, here are some phrases you can use:

e.g. Do you think there will be another major earthquake in San Francisco before the year 2001?

Yes,	I'm almost sure I'm pretty certain there's a very good chance that the chances are that in all probability	there will be.
Yes,	probably. almost certainly. I think so. almost definitely.	

or

No,	I'm almost sure I'm pretty certain in all probability the chances are	there won't be.
No,	probably not. I don't think so. it's highly unlikely. there's very little chance of that happening.	

PRACTICE 2

Work in pairs. Take turns to ask and answer the following questions, expressing probability that the event will or will not happen.

Do you think (that):

1. the Olympic Games in their present form will die out?
2. the U.S.A. will ever have a woman President?
3. there will be an explosion at a nuclear power station?
4. our country will ever manage to send a man to Mars?
5. the average working week will be reduced to 30 hours within the next ten years?

Unit 10: Certainty and Uncertainty

c) How to express uncertainty and doubt

When you are not sure, or doubtful, whether something will happen in the future, here are some phrases you can use:

e.g. Do you think there will be atomic war before the year 2000?

Well,	it's possible, there might be, it could happen, it's not impossible, there's always a chance,	I suppose,
	you never know, of course, no one can say for certain, possibly, perhaps, maybe,	

but	I wouldn't like to say for certain. I'm not really sure. I doubt it. I have my doubts. it's doubtful. it's highly unlikely.

PRACTICE 3

Work in pairs. Take turns to ask and answer the following questions, expressing uncertainty or doubt that the event will happen.

Do you think (that):

1. people will ever live to be at least 150?
2. there will ever be a World Government?
3. cities will be built under the sea?
4. there will be a Third World War by 1990?
5. Africa will become united, with one Government and President for the whole continent?
6. English will become the world language?
7. it will be possible to go on holiday to the moon in the next fifty years?
8. a method will soon be found to detect and prevent earthquakes?

d) How to express ignorance or lack of knowledge

When you have no idea whether or not something will happen in the future, here are some phrases you can use:

e.g. Do you think there'll be a Third World War by 1990?

> I really wouldn't like to say.
> I must admit, I don't know.
> I've (really) no idea.
> I haven't a clue.
> Who knows?
> Your guess is as good as mine.
> How should I know?
> It's impossible to say.

PRACTICE 4

Work in pairs. Take turns to ask and answer the following questions, expressing ignorance or lack of knowledge about whether the event will ever happen.

Do you think (that):

1. nuclear weapons will one day be banned?
2. every home will have its own computer?
3. marriage will die out?
4. there will ever be peace in the world?
5. the world will soon come to an end?

e) How to give reasons for your certainty or uncertainty

When you want to give a reason for your certainty or uncertainty, here are some phrases you can use:

e.g. Why are you so sure that England will win the next World Cup?

Because For the simple reason that		(they haven't lost a match for over two years).
Owing to Mainly due to	the fact that	
Because of On account of	(their unbeaten record over the past two years).	

*Voicing
opinions
Speakers' Corne[r]
Hyde Pa[rk]*

PRACTICE 5

Match up the questions from A with an appropriate reason from B.

A
> Why are you so sure that David won't marry Davina?
> Why are you so certain that there will be another earthquake in San Francisco in the near future?
> Why do you doubt that you'll get the job?
> Why aren't you sure whether or not you'll come with us to Spain next summer?
> Why are you so positive that you'll beat him?
> Why are you so certain that he won't come with us?

B
> Because of my lack of experience.
> Because he told me last week that he was going to break off his engagement.
> Mainly due to the fact that his parents never let him go anywhere.
> On account of scientific evidence.
> For the simple reason that I may have to go into hospital for an operation in July.
> Owing to the fact that I've already beaten him six times in the past year.

Written Practice

Now make your own predictions about the future (up to the year 2001) by completing the following sentences:

1. I'm positive that ....
2. I'm certain that .... (*won't happen*)
3. I'm almost sure that ....
4. I'm pretty certain that .... (*won't happen*)
5. It's possible that ...., but I wouldn't like to say for certain.
6. I suspect that ...., but I'm not really sure.
7. It's possible that ...., but I doubt it.
8. Perhaps ...., but I have my doubts.
9. I really wouldn't like to say if ....
10. It's impossible to say if ....

Unit 10: Certainty and Uncertainty

Dialogue

Practise reading the following dialogue in groups of three. Read the dialogue again, replacing the phrases in **bold** with phrases of similar meaning. Then write out the new dialogue.

A: Do you think England will win the next World Cup?

B: Yes, **of course they will.** Why? Don't you think so, then?

A: Well, **they might, I suppose,** but **I wouldn't like to say for certain.**

C: Yes, I agree. In fact, **I'm almost sure** West Germany will win it.

B: West Germany? No, **definitely not.**

C: Why do you say that?

B: **Because** England have got a much better team, haven't they, Peter?

A: Well, **I really wouldn't like to say.** After all, West Germany have beaten England three times in the past few years.

B: So what? That was in the past. **I'm quite certain** they won't lose this time.

C: Well, **it's possible, I suppose,** but **I have my doubts.**

Group Work

PREDICTING THE FUTURE

Work in groups of three or four.

You are now going to try to make some predictions about life in the year 2001. Use the following types of sentence:

> We're (absolutely sure) that ....
> We're (almost certain) that ....
> It's possible that ....

Think about the following:

    types of transport
    nuclear power
    machines in the home
    medicine
    war or peace?
    fashion
    music
    new discoveries
    types of job
    average earnings

When each group has finished, they read out their predictions to the rest of the class (who can either agree or disagree with them!).

11:
Past Regrets

Simon and Joanna drove out of London to go to a pop concert. On the way home, the car skidded and crashed into a lamp-post. Neither Simon nor Joanna was hurt, but they are now sitting in Simon's flat, still feeling rather shocked.

SIMON: Oh, hell! This is all my fault! If only I'd been driving a bit more carefully.

JOANNA: Now, come on, Simon ... don't take it so badly. It could have happened to anyone. Believe me, no one could have stopped in time. The road was so wet.

SIMON: Yes, that may be, but I shouldn't have been driving so fast in the first place. I was well above the speed-limit. You know I was!

JOANNA: Well, that was just as much my fault as yours, wasn't it?

SIMON: No, Jo, you weren't to blame. I was the one who was driving. You had nothing to do with it.

JOANNA: Yes, I did! I was the one who kept saying I had to be back by midnight, didn't I? If I hadn't kept on about that, do you think you would have been driving so fast? I doubt it very much.

SIMON: Oh, I don't know. Perhaps I would ... perhaps I wouldn't. But I wish we'd left a bit sooner. We could have quite easily. There was no need to go for a meal, really.

JOANNA: Yes, well we weren't to know it would take so long to get served, were we? And anyway, things could have been a lot worse. At least no one was killed.

SIMON: No, but they might have been. *You* might have been killed. And that's what I can't forget.

JOANNA: But you must, Simon! You can't go on blaming yourself like this. It was just one of those things. It happened and there's nothing you can do to change that. So come on ... try to cheer up.

a) How to express past regret

You regret something you did (or didn't do) in the past.

e.g. Situation: A year ago you were offered £10,000 of shares in a new company. You bought them even though your wife/husband told you you were taking a big risk. A week ago, the company went bankrupt and now your shares are virtually worthless.

Here are some ways you could express your regret at having bought the shares (or at not having listened to your wife/husband):

If only I wish	I hadn't I'd never		bought those shares.
	I'd		listened to my wife/husband.
I don't know why I can't think why I'm (really) sorry	I	ever	bought those shares.
		never didn't	listen(ed) to my wife/husband.
I shouldn't have I must have been stupid to have			bought those shares.
I should have I was stupid not to have			listened to my wife/husband.
I (really) regret	ever having		bought those shares.
	not having		listened to my wife/husband.

PRACTICE 1

Make up suitable expressions of regret from the following situations. Try to use as many different phrases as possible.

1. You bought a new stereo a few months ago. You lent it to a friend for the weekend. He had a party and it got broken.
2. You were asked to join Manchester United when you were sixteen, but turned it down to go to university. Now you are unemployed.
3. You bet your holiday savings (£100) on a horse in the Grand National. A friend of yours had told you it couldn't possibly lose. The horse fell at the first fence!

1: Past Regrets

4. When you were younger you broke off your engagement to a girl called Amanda Beswick. Now she is a famous and wealthy film-star.
5. Your house is just about to be pulled down to make way for a new motorway. Although the local council have given you money, you could have got twice as much if you'd sold it last year. But your husband didn't want to sell.
6. You were offered the chance of a partnership in a new cinema in the West End. Your brother told you it was too risky, so you turned down the offer. Now, the cinema is the most popular one in London.

b) How to reply by expressing sympathy

You can reply to an expression of past regret by expressing sympathy:

Don't take it so badly, Don't blame yourself, I know how you must be feeling, but It's not really your fault,	it could have happened to anyone.
	you weren't to know it would happen.

PRACTICE 2

Work in pairs. A expresses past regret, using the words and the pictures below, while B offers some words of sympathy. Try to use as many different phrases as possible.

I regret:

1. rushing out of the house
2. driving carelessly 
3. buying this second-hand car

Unit 11: Past Regrets

4. changing my job

5. not listening to the weather forecast

6. not getting married to him/her

7. not posting the football coupon

8. not selling the house

c) How to reply by expressing general resignation

Ah, well,	that's life.
	these things happen.
	there's nothing you can do about it now.
	just put it down to experience.
	you weren't to know, were you?
	what's done is done.
	it's just one of those things.

PRACTICE 3

Work in pairs. Go through Practice 2 again, but this time B philosophically offers some words of resignation.

Unit 11: Past Regrets

d) How to reply by expressing hope

Still,	I'm sure something will turn up. it could have been a lot worse, couldn't it? perhaps it's not as bad as you think. you might be able to do something yet. you've got to look on the bright side of things.

PRACTICE 4

Work in pairs. Take turns to express past regret, using the words below, and to offer some words of hope. Try to use as many different phrases as possible, and remember to change the verb.

I regret:

1. not taking that job in Africa.
2. lending him the money.
3. not buying that house when we had the chance.
4. speaking to him like that.
5. throwing away the receipt.

What do you think has happened in the above?

e) How to reply by expressing criticism

Well,	all I can say is,	you've only got yourself to blame. I hope you've learned your lesson. I hope you're satisfied now. it's (entirely) your own fault.
	perhaps you'll be more careful in future. perhaps you'll listen (to me) next time. don't say I didn't warn you. I told you so!	

Unit 11: Past Regrets

PRACTICE 5

Work in pairs. Take turns to express past regret, using the words below, and to offer some words of criticism. Try to use as many phrases as possible, and remember to change the verb.

I regret:

1. not selling my shares when I had a chance.
2. not locking the back door.
3. spending so much money.
4. deciding to go to Scotland with him/her.
5. stopping to have a drink.

What do you think has happened in the above?

Written Practice

Fill in the blanks in the following conversations:

1. A: .... sold my car.
   B: .... (*expresses sympathy*)

2. A: .... bought that house in Scotland.
   B: .... (*expresses hope*)

3. A: .... didn't emigrate when I had the chance.
   B: .... (*expresses resignation*)

4. A: .... didn't check the back door before we went out.
   B: .... (*expresses criticism*)

5. A: .... married him when he first asked me.
   B: .... (*expresses hope*)

6. A: .... gone with them to Monte Carlo.
   B: .... (*expresses sympathy*)

7. A: .... asked him for his address.
   B: .... (*expresses resignation*)

8. A: .... gone to see that film.
   B: .... (*expresses sympathy*)

9. A: .... let him talk me into starting up an escort agency.
   B: .... (*expresses criticism*)

10. A: .... worked harder when I was at school.
    B: .... (*expresses criticism*)

Unit 11: Past Regrets

Dialogue

Practise reading the following dialogue in groups of three. Read the dialogue again, replacing the phrases in **bold** with phrases of similar meaning. Then write out the new dialogue. Before starting, read through the following:

Situation: James Thompson's house was burgled at the weekend. He had gone to see some friends even though he wasn't feeling very well at the time. (He had a cold.) The burglar, who got in through an open window, stole some money and a valuable clock. James is talking to two colleagues at work, Sally and Paul.

A: **If only** I'd checked that all the windows were closed, Paul.

B: **Don't blame yourself,** James. **You weren't to know it would happen.**

A: But **I shouldn't have** gone away for the weekend. I had a terrible cold. **I should have** stayed at home.

C: Ah, well, James, **that's life!**

A: And **I wish I'd** sold the clock when the chap offered to buy it last month.

B: Still, **it could have been a lot worse, couldn't it?** At least it's insured.

A: But that's the point! It's not!

C: What? You mean it wasn't insured?

A: No, Sally. The policy had run out and I was too busy to renew it. **I must have been stupid to have** let it lapse like that.

C: Well, James, **all I can say is, you've only got yourself to blame.**

A: I know, I know. Don't rub it in.

Unit 11: Past Regrets

Role-Play

THE DREAM HOUSE

Work in groups of three.
Read the following newspaper article:

Dream house turns into a nightmare

A surprise awaited Mr Peter Pratt and his wife, Samantha, last night when they returned to their new £40,000 'dream house' in Castle Road. It was on fire! Numbed and horrified, they stood by helplessly as firemen tried desperately to contain the blaze. It wasn't until 2.30 a.m. that things were finally under control. But the house, which the Pratts had designed themselves and had only moved into the previous week, was almost completely destroyed.

The fire broke out at approximately 10.15 p.m. when one of the neighbours, Mrs Pry, noticed smoke coming out of the back door. The cause of the fire is believed to have been an automatic coffee percolator which the Pratts had forgotten to switch off, and which had caught fire. According to the manufacturers, these coffee percolators should never be left on for more than an hour at a time.

Unit 11: Past Regrets

Two people are Mr and Mrs Pratt and the other person is a friend of theirs. It is a few days after the fire and they are discussing it with their friend.

Before starting, read through the following account of events on the day of the fire.

TIME	EVENT
2 p.m.	Mrs Pratt's mother brings her daughter an automatic coffee percolator as a moving-in present.
2.20 p.m.	Mrs Pratt tries the new percolator. She throws away the operating instructions without looking at them.
7 p.m.	Mr Pratt suggests they go out for a meal to celebrate having been in the house a whole week. Mrs Pratt asks if they can wait until 9 o'clock because she wants to see her favourite television programme first.
8.30 p.m.	Mr Pratt suggests a cup of tea. Mrs Pratt persuades him to make coffee using the new percolator.
8.45 p.m.	Mrs Pratt makes Mr Pratt another cup of coffee. She forgets to switch off the percolator.
9.05 p.m.	On the way to the restaurant Mrs Pratt remembers that she has left the percolator on. She suggests going back to switch it off but Mr Pratt tells her that it will be all right.
10.45 p.m.	The Pratts leave the restaurant. Mr Pratt notices that he doesn't have much petrol left. He decides to call in at a filling station.
11.00 p.m.	The Pratts find a filling station at last.
11.30 p.m.	The Pratts arrive home. Their house is on fire.

Remember to use expressions of past regret and to respond accordingly. Mr Pratt may think it was Mrs Pratt's fault, and she may think it was his.

Unit 12:
Apologies and Excuses

Sally had arranged to meet Peter after work outside the National Theatre. They were going to see Equus *together. The play began at 7.30 and it is now eight o'clock. Sally is about to give up and go home when Peter arrives.*

SALLY: And about time, too! I've been standing here since half past seven! Where on earth have you been?

PETER: I'm terribly sorry I'm late, Sally, but I just couldn't help it. I got here as soon as I could.

SALLY: Well, it's not soon enough, is it? It's too late to go in now – the play's already started!

PETER: I know ... and I'm sorry but ...

SALLY: It's all very well saying you're sorry but you know how much I was looking forward to seeing it.

PETER: I know and ...

SALLY: I've been waiting to see it all week! Do you realize that? All week!

PETER: Look, Sally, just give me a chance to explain – please! You'll see it wasn't really my fault.

SALLY: All right, then. Explain! Go on! But it had better be good!

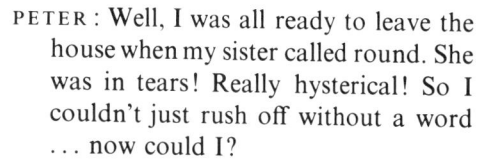

PETER: Well, I was all ready to leave the house when my sister called round. She was in tears! Really hysterical! So I couldn't just rush off without a word ... now could I?

SALLY: Go on!

PETER: Yes ... well ... I invited her in and she told me that John – that's her boyfriend – had been knocked down and was critically ill. Honestly, Sally, I've never seen my sister in such a state. So I stayed with her until she calmed down. Then I came here as quickly as I could.

SALLY: Oh ... I see.

PETER: I am sorry, Sally, but I couldn't have left her like that, could I?

SALLY: No, I suppose not. But you could have phoned me at work, surely? It wouldn't have taken you a minute. I'd have understood.

PETER: I did try, but you'd just left. I am sorry about the play – really I am. I know how much you wanted to see it.

SALLY: Yes – well, never mind. We can always see it some other time.

PETER: Yes, of course we can.

SALLY: And Peter?

PETER: Yes?

SALLY: I'm sorry for the way I snapped at you.

PETER: Oh, that's all right. I understand. I'd have been just as angry in your place.

The National Theatre on the South Bank

Unit 12: Apologies and Excuses

a) How to apologize

When you apologize to someone for something you have done or failed to do, here are some phrases you can use:

I'm	awfully terribly dreadfully ever so	sorry, (John), but	(I'm afraid)

I've lost I seem to have mislaid	(that book you lent me).
I forgot to I wasn't able to I couldn't	(post the football coupon).

b) How to accept an apology and give reassurance

When you are ready to accept an apology, and want to reassure the person that it does not matter, you can say:

Oh,	that's all right. don't worry about it. it doesn't matter. don't let it worry you. don't give it another thought. never mind. not to worry. forget it! it can't be helped.	(It was an old book, anyway.) (We didn't win anything, anyway.)

PRACTICE 1

Work in pairs. A apologizes for something he/she has done or failed to do and B accepts the apology.

A apologizes for:

1. breaking B's watch.
2. dropping ash on B's carpet.
3. scratching the record B had lent him/her.
4. damaging B's roses.
5. knocking over B's vase.
6. not sending that parcel after all.
7. not turning up last night.
8. not having phoned last night.

B replies that:

it was an old one, anyway.
he/she was going to shampoo it soon, anyway.
he/she never really liked it, anyway.

they were dying, anyway.
he/she couldn't stand it, anyway.
he/she can do it this afternoon.
they had enough people, anyway.
it wasn't really very important.

c) How to show anger, displeasure or disappointment (1)

At what a person has done:

Oh,	you haven't, have you? don't say that! how could you (do that)? no!	(It was a library book!)
You've done what?		

At what a person has failed to do:

Oh,	you didn't	did you? forget, surely?
	(John), how could you forget?	
	you	could have were (able to)	surely?
You	couldn't? weren't able to?	
Oh, no! Don't say that!		

Unit 12: Apologies and Excuses

> (That means we've lost a fortune!)
> (Well, it's a bit late to be sorry now!)
> (Thanks to you we've just lost £150,000!)

PRACTICE 2

Work in pairs. A apologizes for something he/she has done or failed to do and B shows anger.

A apologizes for:

1. running into the back of B's car.
2. losing the book B lent him/her.
3. damaging B's stereo.
4. breaking a string on B's guitar.
5. forgetting to meet B's sister last night.
6. not being able to post the letter B had given him/her.
7. not turning up for the match.
8. not phoning last night.

B replies that:

he/she only bought it last week.
he/she needed it for the exam.
it cost £500.
he/she is giving a concert tonight.
she was very annoyed.
A knew how important it was.

they lost 10–1.
he/she stayed up waiting.

d) How to give excuses

When you apologize and wish to offer an excuse or reason, here are some phrases you can use:

For something you've done:

I'm (terribly) sorry (I've spilled ink on your carpet), I'm (awfully) sorry this has happened, I'm (ever so) sorry about (your carpet), Sorry about this,	but	it wasn't really my fault. I couldn't help it. there was very little I could do about it. the fault's not entirely mine. I'm not entirely to blame. it wasn't deliberate. it was an accident.

> Someone had forgotten to screw on the top of the ink bottle!

For something you failed to do:

I'm (terribly) sorry I didn't (phone) / Sorry for not having (phoned)	last night,

but I	wasn't able to, couldn't,	I'm afraid.	(My phone was out of order.)

e) How to accept an excuse

When someone makes an excuse for something he/she has done (or failed to do), you can accept the excuse as follows:

Oh,	don't	worry (about it). let it worry you. give it another thought.	It could have happened to anyone. I'm sure it wasn't your fault. These things happen. You weren't to know (someone had forgotten to screw on the top of the ink bottle).
	it's all right. forget it!		I (quite) understand. I know you wouldn't have let me down deliberately.

Unit 12: Apologies and Excuses

PRACTICE 3

Work in pairs. A apologizes for something he/she has done or failed to do, and offers an excuse or reason, using the situations below. B accepts A's apology.

1. You have spilled your drink over someone's dress. It happened when her cat jumped on your lap.

2. You have knocked over a vase. It was on the edge of the table.

3. You have lost someone's book. Your mother accidentally threw it in the dustbin when she was tidying up.

4. You were supposed to go to a party last night but your cousins from Wales arrived unexpectedly and invited you out to a restaurant with them. You last saw them three years ago.

5. You told a friend last Saturday that you would pick him/her up in the afternoon and take him/her to a football match. But you had a car crash on the way to meet him/her.

6. You promised your mother that you would go round and see her yesterday afternoon after work. But you were asked to work overtime and didn't finish until 8 o'clock. So you went home.

7. You didn't turn up for an interview at 8 o'clock this morning because you forgot to set your alarm clock last night and didn't wake up until 10 o'clock.

f) How to show anger or displeasure (2)

At what the person has done:

It's all very well saying	it wasn't your fault, you couldn't help it, there was very little you could do about it, the fault's not entirely yours, you weren't entirely to blame, it wasn't deliberate, it was an accident,

but	how am I going to get the stain off my carpet? I only had the carpet cleaned last week! it's a brand new carpet! what about my carpet? it was you who knocked over the bottle!

At what the person has failed to do:

It's all very well saying you	couldn't, weren't able to,

but	surely you could have / you could at least have / why couldn't you have	used a public phone box. phoned from your neighbour's. tried ringing from a public phone box?
	why on earth didn't you (phone from your neighbour's)?	
	(it just so happens that I stayed up until midnight waiting for your call!)	

PRACTICE 4

Go through Practice 3 again, this time showing anger at what the person has done, using the words below. Try to use as many different phrases as possible.
1. I only bought this dress yesterday!
2. That vase happens to be over 100 years old!
3. It was a book I borrowed from the library!
4. called me and explained what had happened
5. I missed the match waiting for you to pick me up!
6. ring me to say you were working late
7. remembered to set your alarm clock

Unit 12: Apologies and Excuses

Written Practice 1

Complete the following dialogues:

1. A: I'm .... I've lost that record you lent me.
   B: .... (*accepts the apology*)

2. A: I'm .... I knocked over that small statue.
   B: .... (*shows anger*)

3. A: .... forgot to give Mary your message.
   B: .... (*accepts the apology*)

4. A: .... wasn't able to give you a lift home last night.
   B: .... (*shows anger*)

5. A: .... didn't come round last night but I ....
   B: ....! It just so happens I turned down an invitation to go to a party because of you!

6. A: .... for not having told you where the party was but I ....
   B: ....! Thanks to you, I walked around for miles.

7. A: Sorry about this, but .... Someone pushed me.
   B: .... (*accepts the apology*)

8. A: I'm .... my dog's damaged your roses but .... He was chasing your cat.
   B: .... (*shows anger*) but ....

9. A: .... didn't turn up last night but I had to ....
   B: .... (*accepts the apology*)

10. A: .... for not having .... but .... I had to take my mother to the hospital.
    B: .... (*shows anger*)

g) How to question someone further about what they have done

When someone apologizes for something he/she has done (e.g. I'm terribly sorry, John, but I'm afraid I've left your book on the train), and you cannot fully understand how he/she could have done it, you can ask one of the following questions:

But how	on earth in the world in heaven's name	did you manage to was it possible to	leave it behind? just leave it there?
		could you have left it on the train? could it have happened?	

h) How to reply by confessing ignorance and astonishment

(Look,)	don't ask me. I've no idea. I haven't a clue. I really don't know.	It just happened, that's all.
	Your guess is as good as mine. I really haven't the faintest idea.	(All I know is that I had it when I got on the train and it was missing when I left the station.)

Goodness (only) knows! It beats me! Who knows? I wish I knew!	(It was in my bag when I got on the train.)

so	I really	can't	think imagine	what happened!
		haven't	a clue the faintest idea	
		have no idea		

PRACTICE 5

Work in pairs. A demands explanations, using the words given. B expresses ignorance and astonishment at what has happened.

1. knock over the vase?    2. mislay my record?    3. run over my dog?

Unit 12: Apologies and Excuses

4. burn a hole in my carpet?    5. lose your way?    6. break a plate?

i) How to reply by trying to offer an explanation

I don't know, really, (but)	it might have it could have	(dropped out of my bag), I suppose.
	it's possible that perhaps	(it dropped out of my bag).

The only explanation that I can think of is that I Well, I must have	(left it on the seat when I got off the train).
As I was (getting off the train) it must have (fallen out of my bag).	

PRACTICE 6

Go through Practice 5 again, but this time B tries to offer an explanation for what has happened, using the words below. Try to use as many different phrases as possible.

1. caught it with my bag
2. left it at some party or other
3. run out from behind a parked car
4. fallen out of the ashtray
5. taken the wrong turning somewhere
6. hands were wet

j) How to question someone further about what they failed to do

When someone has failed to do something and apologizes for not having done it (e.g. I'm sorry I didn't turn up last night but I wasn't able to, I'm afraid) and you would like further details, you can ask one of the following questions:

But	why (on earth) didn't you wasn't it possible to	(let me know)?
	surely you could have couldn't you have you could at least have why couldn't you have	(phoned to let me know)?

k) How to reply by saying you did not think of doing it

Yes,	I could have, I suppose, I suppose so, but	I just didn't think about it (that's all).
Well, to be (perfectly) honest		it (just) didn't occur to me.

PRACTICE 7

Work in pairs. A asks B why he/she didn't think of doing something, using the words below. B admits that it had not occurred to him/her to do it. Change the verb if necessary and try to ask and answer in as many different ways as possible.

1. get a taxi?
2. tell them not to come?
3. borrow some money from someone?
4. phone up and explain?
5. catch the next train?
6. leave a message with my mother?

l) How to reply by offering an excuse

Well,	I did think about it I was going to I would have I know I should have	but only	(there just wasn't enough time).

Unit 12: Apologies and Excuses

or

No,	I couldn't, I'm afraid, it wasn't possible, I'm afraid, not really,

because for the simple reason that	(there just wasn't enough time).

PRACTICE 8

Go through Practice 7 again. This time B offers an excuse or reason for not having done what was suggested, using the words below:

1. I didn't have enough money.
2. They're not on the phone.
3. I didn't know who to ask.
4. My phone was out of order.
5. There wasn't another one until midnight.
6. I thought I'd see you at the pub.

Written Practice 2

Complete the following dialogues:

1. A: I'm .... but I've broken a plate.
   B: But how ....?
   A: .... (*says he has no idea*)

2. A: I'm .... but I seem to have mislaid that book you lent me.
   B: But how ....?
   A: I don't know really. .... (*possible explanation*)

3. A: I'm .... but I wasn't able to post that letter you gave me.
   B: But ....?
   A: .... (*says it didn't occur to him*)

4. A: .... but I couldn't get hold of Sally last night.
   B: But ....?
   A: No, ... because ....

Dialogue

Practise reading the following dialogue in pairs. Read the dialogue again, replacing the phrases in **bold** with phrases of similar meaning. Then write out the new dialogue.

A: Look, **I'm sorry I didn't** turn up for the match yesterday, but **I couldn't, I'm afraid.**

B: Well, it's **a bit late to be** sorry now, isn't it?

A: I know that, but **it wasn't really my fault,** you know.

B: It's all very well saying **it wasn't your fault,** but thanks to you we lost 10–1!

A: Yes, I heard, and I'm sorry, but I was on my way to the match when I ran into the back of a lorry.

B: How, **in heaven's name, did you manage to** do that?

A: **I haven't a clue.** I was driving along when suddenly it braked and – wham! – I went into the back of it.

B: Were you hurt?

A: Fortunately, no. But my car's a complete write-off!

B: But **why on earth didn't you** phone to let us know?

A: **Well, to be perfectly honest, it just didn't occur to me** at the time.

B: But **couldn't you have got** a lift to the match – even if you only got there at half-time?

A: Well, **I did think about it,** but I wasn't exactly in the mood for playing football, you know. Anyway, by the time the police had finished with me the match was over!

Unit 12: Apologies and Excuses

Role-Play

EXCUSES

For the whole class.
Each student in the group is given one of the following situations:

1. You were two hours late for class this morning.
2. You have lost £5, which a friend asked you to keep for him/her.
3. You borrowed a friend's car last night and have damaged it.
4. You forgot to post a football coupon for the group. (You do the pools together.) You have got 24 points!
5. You were supposed to meet your boyfriend/girlfriend outside the cinema last night. You never turned up.
6. You have not done your homework.
7. A window was broken in the classroom during the coffee-break. You left the room five minutes after everyone else.
8. You took a friend's dog for a walk in the park. You have come back without his/her dog.
9. You turned up very late for an important meeting yesterday.

Each student has to think of a good excuse or reason for having done the above.
When everyone is ready, students take it in turns to apologize and give their excuses or reasons to the rest of the group. The group listens and either accepts or rejects the excuse. The group can also ask further questions, e.g. But why didn't you let her know? etc.
At the end, the group decides whether the person was to blame or not.

Unit 13:
Socializing (2)

Sally is sitting on a bus, on her way to work. A friend of Peter's from college – Brian Southgate – gets on and sits down beside her. It is raining.

SALLY: 'Morning, Brian.
BRIAN: 'Morning, Sally. How are you feeling today?
SALLY: Fine, thanks, Brian. And you?
BRIAN: Oh, pretty good, thanks. Shocking weather, isn't it?
SALLY: Yes, terrible. Not exactly what you'd expect for July, is it?
BRIAN: No, it's not. Been a poor summer this year.
SALLY: Yes, it certainly has.
  [*a slight pause*]
BRIAN: How's Peter now? Has he got over the flu yet?
SALLY: Oh, he's much better, thanks. The doctor says he'll be all right in a couple of days.
BRIAN: Oh, I am pleased to hear that.
SALLY: Yes, it is good news.
BRIAN: Talking of news – have you heard about Claire?
SALLY: No. What's happened?
BRIAN: Well, I haven't seen her since the end of term, so I'm not sure if it's true, but apparently, she's failed her finals.
SALLY: Oh, no! Poor Claire! She must be so upset.
BRIAN: I don't expect so. She's already found a job in a jazz club.
SALLY: You're not serious, are you?
BRIAN: Oh, yes. She's always liked jazz. And I hated it. Maybe that's why she'd hardly ever come out with me.
SALLY: [*laughing*] Could be.
BRIAN: Ah! Here's my stop. [*He gets up.*] By the way, are you going to Simon's party on Saturday?
SALLY: Yes, I expect so.
BRIAN: Good. I'll probably see you there, then. Well, cheerio and give my regards to Peter.
SALLY: Yes, I will. Cheerio.
  [*Brian gets off.*]

Unit 13: Socializing (2)

a) How to greet an acquaintance

When you meet a friend (or someone you know) in the street, you can greet him/her with one of the following phrases:

Hello, (Good) morning, Afternoon, Evening,	(Mr South). (Mrs Thompson). (Alan). (Pam).	How are	you? things?
		How's	life?

b) How to reply to a greeting

When a friend (or someone you know) greets you, you can reply with one of the following phrases:

Oh,	hello,	(Mr South), (Mrs Thompson), (Alan), (Pam),	very well, fine, all right, pretty good, not too bad,	thanks.	And you?

The first person now replies to your: *And you?*, using one of the above phrases, but not the same one as you used.

PRACTICE 1

Work in pairs. Take turns to greet one another and reply to a greeting, using the situations below. Try to use as many different phrases as possible.

1. Charlotte meets Sally in the street.
2. John meets Mrs Brown on the bus.
3. Rita meets Mr Collins at the pub.
4. Alan meets Peter in the park.
5. Clive meets Lynne on the beach.
6. Mr Davies meets Miss Love in the lift.

c) How to make a comment about the weather

English people, when they meet, nearly always make some comment about the weather. Here are some phrases you can use when talking about:

Good weather:

(It's)	nice nice and warm nice and sunny nice and hot very nice quite mild hot beautiful	(today),	isn't it?
	(a) lovely day, marvellous weather,		

Bad weather:

(It's)	a bit rather very	cold wet cloudy overcast windy	(today),	isn't it?
	(a) shocking day, terrible weather,			
	not very	nice, promising,		is it?
(It)	looks like rain, doesn't it?			

d) How to reply to a comment about the weather

People talk about the weather in order to be sociable. So if a person makes a comment about the weather, you should usually agree with him/her. Here are some phrases you can use when replying to a comment about:

Unit 13: Socializing (2)

Good weather:

Yes,	beautiful. very nice. wonderful. very pleasant. lovely. marvellous.	And they say it's going to stay warm for the next couple of days. We could do with some nice weather for a change. It's about time we had some sun. Let's hope it keeps like this. Makes a change from all the rain we've had lately.

Bad weather:

Yes,	horrible. dreadful. terrible. awful. shocking.	And they say it's going to stay like this until the weekend. Good for the garden, though. I'll be glad when the summer comes. It's about time we had some sun. No sign of it changing, either.
No, terrible.		
Yes, it does.		

PRACTICE 2

Now take turns to greet someone and to make a comment about the weather, using the situations below. The other person returns the greeting and also replies to the comment about the weather.

1. Tom meets Bob in the park. It is 30°C.
2. Pam meets Susan at the bus stop. It is raining.
3. Mr Brown meets Charlotte outside the post office. They are both wearing thick coats, gloves and scarves.
4. Tom meets Mr Smith in the street. Tom is wearing a T-shirt and dark glasses.
5. Mr Collins meets Miss Allbright on the way to the office. There are heavy black clouds in the sky.
6. Julie meets Roger at the pub at lunchtime. It is very windy.

e) How to ask after a friend or relative

When you want to ask your friend about his/her family or friends, you can use one of the following phrases:

How's	your (brother) these days? your (wife)? (Betty)? your family?
Family Children (Betty)	all right? O.K.?

f) How to reply to an inquiry about a friend or relative

When you reply to an inquiry about a member of your family or a close friend, you can use one of the following phrases:

He's They're She's	fine, all right, very well, pretty good, not too bad,	thanks.	And	(Betty)? yours?
Yes (pretty good), thanks.				

The first person now replies to your inquiry with one of the above phrases.

g) How to respond to a piece of good news

Sometimes, when you ask after a friend or relative you are given a piece of good news or bad news. When you are given good news, you can use one of the following phrases:

Unit 13: Socializing (2)

e.g.

> A: How's (Betty)?
> B: (She)'s fine, thanks. In fact, (she)'s just had her first novel accepted.

Has (she)? Well, I never! Really? Gosh!	How	marvellous! wonderful! tremendous! super!
	That's	good news! terrific! great!
	What	luck! a surprise!

I must remember to congratulate (her) when I see (her). You must congratulate (her) from me. You must be very proud of (her). (She) certainly deserves it!		
(She) must be feeling very	pleased with (herself). happy. excited.	

PRACTICE 3

Work in pairs. A asks about someone and B replies by giving a piece of good news about that person, using the situations below. A reacts accordingly. Try to use as many different phrases as possible.

1. Your brother, William, has just got married.
2. Your mother has just won £150,000 on the football pools.
3. Your sister, Kate, has just been given the leading part in a new West End musical.
4. Your younger brother, John, has just passed his G.C.E. O-level exams.
5. Your cousin, Rita, has been offered a very good job with the B.B.C.
6. Your father has had a book of poems accepted for publication.

h) How to respond to bad news

> A: How's (your brother)?
> B: Not too good, I'm afraid. (He)'s just lost (his) job.

Has (he)? Oh,	I'm (ever so) / I am	sorry to hear that.
	what that's	a pity. / a shame. / a bit of bad luck.
	but that's how	awful. / dreadful. / terrible.

Oh, no!	(He) hasn't, has (he)? What bad luck! I had no idea.
	Poor (Tom). / Poor thing.

You really must tell me if there's anything I can do (to help).
Is there anything I can do (to help)?
(He) certainly doesn't deserve it.
Things always seem to happen to (him).
And (he) was so (happy) when I last saw (him), too!

(He) must be so	unhappy. disappointed. worried. fed up. miserable. upset.

PRACTICE 4

Work in pairs. A asks about someone and B replies by giving a piece of bad news about that person, using the situations given. A reacts accordingly.

1. Your sister, Pam, has just been rushed to hospital with suspected polio.

Unit 13: Socializing (2)

2. Your friend, Glen, has just broken his leg.
3. Brian's mother has just died.
4. Your parents' house was burgled last weekend.
5. Your friend, Sue, has just been given the sack.
6. Your sister, Janet, has failed to get a place at university.

i) How to introduce a piece of news

When you want to introduce a piece of news you have recently heard about someone you both know, here are some phrases you can use:

By the way, Incidentally,	have you heard	the latest? about (Janet)?
	you've heard	about (Janet), I expect. what they're saying about (Janet), haven't you?
	you know what (Janet)'s (gone and) done, I suppose. you'll never guess what I heard this morning. guess what I found out this morning?	
	what do you think about (Janet), then? wasn't it strange about (Janet), eh? a bit of a surprise about (Janet), don't you think?	

j) How to express interest in a piece of news

No,	I don't think so. I've no idea. I haven't heard a thing.	What's happened? What? What's up?
	what?	
What? Oh, do tell me!		
(Janet)?	What do you mean? What's happened, then? What on earth's happened to (her)?	

138

k) How to pass on a piece of news

When you want to pass on a piece of news, here are some phrases you can use:

Well,	don't spread it around, but and this is strictly off the record, just between ourselves, and this is confidential,
	I'm not sure if saying it's true but

it	appears / seems	that	
apparently / according to (Elsie), / there's a rumour going round that / from what I've heard,			(she's given in her notice).

PRACTICE 5

Work in pairs. A introduces and passes on a piece of news, using the situations below. B hasn't heard anything about the person concerned. Try to use as many different phrases as possible.

1. You have just heard that your boss, Mr Thompson, is leaving at Christmas to become a priest.
2. You have just found out from your friend, Mabel, that Tom Grant has been given the sack.
3. You have just been told by your boss, Mrs O'Sullivan, that the firm is going bankrupt.
4. There is a rumour going about that the new headmaster at the school, Mr Gaymore, is going to reintroduce caning.
5. You heard today that Sheila Steele, the boss's secretary, has been dismissed for stealing from petty cash.

Unit 13: Socializing (2)

There are several ways you can react to a piece of news:

l) How to react by expressing surprise

Well, I never! Good heavens!	That is a surprise! Who would have thought it? That's (absolutely) incredible! That's a turn-up for the book, isn't it?

m) How to react by expressing disbelief

No!	You're	joking, pulling my leg, having me on,	aren't you? surely?
		not serious, are you?	
	(She)'s not, is she? I don't believe it! It's not possible, surely?		
Come off it! Not (Janet)! What – (Janet)?	It can't be true. You must be wrong – surely? I find that very hard to believe(, I must say).		

n) How to react by expressing lack of surprise

Well,	it doesn't surprise me (one bit). I'm not really surprised (, you know). it was to be expected, wasn't it? what do you expect? why not? these things happen, don't they? I always thought (she looked unhappy here).	(She often said she was fed up.) (She didn't get the job she wanted, after all.)

PRACTICE 6

Work in pairs. A passes on a piece of news, using the words given. B doesn't believe what he/she hears. Try to use as many different phrases as possible.

e.g.

> A: Well, *I'm not sure if it's true but it appears that* Janet's thinking of giving in her notice.
> B: *Good heavens! That is a surprise!*

1. Peter Thompson's wife has just written a full-length novel.
2. Mr Blake has been awarded the O.B.E.
3. Viola Kemp has been given the job.
4. Graham has broken off his engagement to Cathy.
5. We're being taken over by an American company.

PRACTICE 7

Work in pairs. A passes on a piece of news, using the words given. B doesn't believe what he/she hears. Try to use as many different phrases as possible.

e.g.

> A: Well, *don't spread it around, but apparently* Janet's thinking of giving in her notice.
> B: *No! I don't believe it!*

1. June Warren has just inherited a fortune from her father.
2. Mr Bryan lost £10,000 on the stock market recently. 
3. Bob Brown punched Mr Gray in the face.

Unit 13: Socializing (2)

4. Jane and David are going to get married.

5. Tom's failed his A-level exams.

PRACTICE 8

Now go through Practice 7 again, but this time B is not in the least surprised, and answers using the words below:

e.g.

> A: Well, *I'm not saying it's true, mind you, but according to Elsie,* Janet's given in her notice.
> B: Well, *it doesn't surprise me one bit. She always seemed unhappy here, didn't she?*

1. Her father always was a good businessman.
2. He's always losing money on the stock market.
3. Mr Gray always treated him very rudely.
4. They've been keen on each other for a long time.
5. He never did any work.

o) How to take your leave

When you feel it is time to go, you can use one of the following phrases:

Well,	I must be off now. I (really) can't stay (any longer). I must be getting along. better be going, I suppose. be seeing you, then.	(I've got to catch the shops before they close.)	Good-bye. Bye-bye. Cheerio. So long. 'Bye.

p) How to respond to a farewell greeting

When a person says good-bye, you can reply:

Yes,	I must go, too. I'd better be going, too. I suppose it's time I (went home), too. see you (at the match), then. be seeing you. fine. O.K.		Good-bye. Bye-bye. Cheerio. So long. 'Bye.

q) How to send someone your regards, and how to reply

When you say good-bye, it is quite common to ask the person you have been talking to to give your regards to his/her wife, boyfriend, etc. If you wish to do this, here are some phrases you can use:

Give my regards to Regards to Remember me to Love to	(John). your (wife). the family.	and reply:	Yes,	of course. O.K. I will. thanks.

PRACTICE 9

Work in pairs. A takes his leave, using the reasons below. B replies and asks A to give his/her regards to someone, shown in brackets.

1. I've got to catch a bus. (*the family*)
2. I must be at the lecture in ten minutes. (*Tom*)
3. I'm meeting Alan in ten minutes. (*him*)
4. I've still got a lot of shopping to do. (*Patricia*)
5. I'm picking my mother up outside Woolworth's at 2.30. (*the boys*)
6. I've got to be back at work in five minutes. (*mother*)

Unit 13: Socializing (2)

PRACTICE 10

Match up the phrases from A with an appropriate response from B.

A
1. 'Morning, Tom. How are you?
2. William's just got married.
3. It appears that John's moving back to Scotland.
4. How's the family?
5. Well, I really must be home by six. 'Bye.
6. Nice today, isn't it?
7. By the way, you've heard about Mr Brown, I expect.
8. I've just heard that Mr Green's going to give us all a £10-a-week pay rise.
9. How's Belinda?
10. Terrible weather, isn't it?
11. Pam's just failed her exam.
12. Remember me to Tom.

B
1. Good heavens! That is a surprise!
2. Yes, of course.
3. Yes, shocking. I'll be glad when the summer comes.
4. Really? That's great! You must congratulate him from me.
5. Oh, fine, thanks. And you?
6. No, I don't think so. What's happened?
7. Yes, beautiful. Let's hope it keeps like this.
8. Yes, I must go, too. Cheerio.
9. Oh, they're all right, thanks. And yours?
10. Well, I'm not really surprised, you know. He was never happy down here.
11. She's fine, thanks.
12. Oh, what a shame! She must be so upset.

Written Practice

Complete the following dialogues:

1. A: ...., Mrs Brown. ....?
   B: .... thanks. ....?
   A: Oh, ...

2. A: .... today, isn't it? (*good weather*)
   B: Yes, ...

3. A: .... (*bad weather*)
   B: ....

4. A: .... your mother?
   B: .... thanks. In fact she won £2,000 in a competition last weekend.
   A: ....

5. A: .... Tom?
   B: ...., I'm afraid. He'll probably have to have an operation.
   A: ....

6. A: ...., heard the latest?
   B: ....?
   A: Well, ... but .... Susan's just been given a new car.
   B: .... (*shows surprise*)

7. A: ...., guess what I found out this morning?
   B: ....
   A: Well, ..., it seems that ....
   B: .... (*shows disbelief*)

8. A: ...., what do you think about Robert, then?
   B: Robert? ....?
   A: Well, ... he's got lung cancer.
   B: .... (*shows lack of surprise*) That's what happens when you smoke forty cigarettes a day!

9. A: Well, ... I've got to catch the shops before they close.
   B: Yes, ... 'Bye. And .... Tom.
   A: Yes, ...

Unit 13: Socializing (2)

Dialogue

Practise reading the following dialogue in pairs. Read the dialogue again, replacing the phrases in **bold** with phrases of similar meaning. Then write out the new dialogue.

A: **'Morning,** Peter. **How are you?**

B: **Fine,** thanks, John. And you?

A: Oh, **I'm all right. Nice and warm** today, isn't it?

B: Yes, **beautiful. And they say it's going to stay warm until the end of next week.**

A: Well, I hope so. Could do with some nice weather for a change.

B: Yes, you're right there. **Family O.K.?**

A: **Yes, they're fine,** thanks. And yours?

B: Well, Sally's not too good at the moment. Her mother was rushed to hospital last week, you know.

A: Oh, **I am sorry to hear that. She must be so upset.**

B: Yes, she is.
   [pause]

A: **By the way, have you heard about** the professor?

B: **No, I don't think so. What's happened?**

A: Well, **I'm not saying it's true, mind you, but there's a rumour going round that** he's leaving.

B: **Come off it! It can't be true!** Not the professor! He was here for life, I thought.

A: Well, that's what they say. Anyway, **I must be off now.** Got to catch the train home. **Cheerio!**

B: Yes, **I'd better be going, too. Cheerio!** Oh, and **give my regards to** your wife, won't you?

A: Yes, **I will.** Cheerio!

St Thomas's Hospital, London

Role-Play

A FRIENDLY CHAT

Work in pairs. In this role-play you meet a friend (or someone you know quite well) and stop for a chat.

The chat should include:

1. Greeting one another	Hello, Mr ... How are you?
2. Comments on the weather	It's a nice day today, isn't it?
3. Health inquiries about a close friend or relative	How's (your daughter)? She's ...
4. A piece of gossip	By the way, have you heard about ...?
5. A farewell greeting	'Bye then. And give my regards to ...

Before you start, read through the notes on page 184 (Person A) and page 188 (Person B).

When you have done the role-play once, change roles and do it again. This time Person A reads 'Role-Play 2' on page 189, and Person B reads 'Role-Play 2' on page 184.

Unit 14: Asking For and Giving Information (2)

Simon lives in a bedsitter just off Wigmore Street. Last night, at about nine o'clock, someone broke into the landlord's bedroom on the ground floor and stole some valuable jewellery. (The landlady was out playing bingo.) A policeman has called round to interview the people living in the house. He is now talking to Simon.

POLICEMAN: Now, sir, I wonder if you'd mind telling me where you were yesterday evening?
SIMON: Certainly. I went to the pictures – the Plaza.
POLICEMAN: Alone, sir?
SIMON: Yes, alone.
POLICEMAN: I see. And could you tell me the name of the film you saw?
SIMON: Yes, it was *La Cuisine*.
POLICEMAN: Sorry, sir? What was the name again?
SIMON: *La Cuisine*. It was a French film.
POLICEMAN: Did you say it was a French film, sir?
SIMON: Yes, that's right.
POLICEMAN: I see. And after the film finished, you came home, did you, sir?
SIMON: Yes, I did.
POLICEMAN: At about what time was that, sir?
SIMON: Oh ... 10.30 ... quarter to eleven ... I'm not sure exactly.
POLICEMAN: Did anyone see you come in?
SIMON: No, not to my knowledge.
POLICEMAN: So you were out of the house all evening?
SIMON: That's right. From 7.30 anyway.
POLICEMAN: I see. Er ... I hope you don't mind my asking this, sir, but you haven't been in trouble with the police before, have you?

SIMON: What on earth do you mean, have I been in trouble with the police?
POLICEMAN: Just routine, sir. We have to ask everyone this.
SIMON: Well, I most certainly have not. Do you think *I* did the burglary or something? Is that what you're trying to say?
POLICEMAN: No, of course not, sir. It's just that we have to interview everyone who has access to the house. Now, just one or two more questions I'd like to ask before I go and have a chat with the landlord and the landlady ...

a) How to ask questions politely

Sometimes, instead of asking a question directly, especially in more formal situations when you do not know the person you are talking to, people introduce a question with a polite phrase. Here are some polite phrases you can use when asking a question:

Would you / I wonder if you'd	mind telling me	
Could you tell me / Do you think you could tell me / Would you be good enough to tell me		(why you applied for this job)?
I wonder if	I might ask / you could tell me	
May I ask		

PRACTICE 1

Work in pairs. A asks B polite questions, using the words below. B gives an appropriate answer. Try to use as many different phrases as you can.

Ask B:

1. why he/she applied for this job.
2. what sort of salary he/she expects.
3. how far it is to the station.
4. who that man is over there.
5. where the manager is.
6. the way to the sales department.
7. how much he/she paid for his/her house.
8. when he/she last saw a doctor.
9. what he/she thinks the job entails.
10. when he/she would be free to see you.

Unit 14: Asking For and Giving Information (2)

b) How to ask awkward or embarrassing questions

When it is necessary to ask someone a question which might make him/her feel awkward or embarrassed, here are some phrases you can use:

I hope you don't mind me asking this, I'm sorry to have to ask this, I hope you won't take this the wrong way, I don't like asking this, I don't quite know how to put this, Perhaps I shouldn't really ask this, I know it's none of my business really, You don't have to answer this if you don't want to,	but	(you haven't been to prison at any time, have you)?

There are several ways you can reply to an awkward or embarrassing question:

c) How to reply by giving a direct answer

Yes,	I have, I do know,	actually. as a matter of fact.	
Well,	as a matter of fact, if you really must know,	I have. I do.	
No,	of course	not. I haven't. I don't.	
	I most certainly	haven't. don't.	

PRACTICE 2

Work in pairs. A asks awkward or embarrassing questions as politely as possible, using the words given. B gives a direct answer.

1. Were you sacked from your last job?
2. Did you phone up my wife/husband last night?

3. Do you realize everyone in the office is furious with you?
4. Are you really only thirty-four?
5. Did you realize that I could hear everything you were saying?

d) How to reply by evading the question or refusing to answer

Well,	I'd rather not answer that, if you don't mind. I'm sorry, but I don't really think that's any of your business. you don't really expect me to answer that, do you? I'm not sure I really want to answer that.
(Prison)? (Married)?	What on earth do you mean? What are you talking about? I don't follow you, I'm afraid.

PRACTICE 3

Work in pairs. A asks awkward or embarrassing questions, using the words below. B tries to evade the question or refuses to answer it.

Ask B:

1. if he/she realized that he/she had upset you by that remark.
2. if he/she knows about his/her brother's dreadful behaviour.
3. if he/she has ever been in trouble with the police.
4. if he/she has false teeth.
5. if he/she took £5 from petty cash without signing for it.

e) How to reply by showing anger, offence or indignation

What if	I have? I do?	What business is it of yours (I'd like to know)? What has it got to do with you?
Mind your own business! I really can't see that's any of your business! What on earth do you mean(, have I been to prison)? How dare you ask that!		

Unit 14: Asking For and Giving Information (2)

PRACTICE 4

Go through Practice 3 again, but this time B replies showing anger, offence or indignation. Try to use as many different phrases as possible.

f) How to question a person again to seek confirmation

When you think something was said but you are not absolutely sure, and would like to have it confirmed, you can ask in one of the following ways:

You did say	you were married, you came from Brighton, your name was Charles,	didn't you?
Did you say	you lived in Brighton? your husband was an architect? I could see you on Friday?	

g) How to reply by confirming what was said

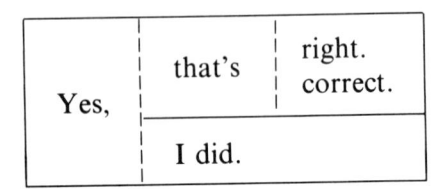

Yes,	that's	right. correct.
	I did.	

PRACTICE 5

Work in pairs. A asks B questions seeking confirmation, using the situations below. B confirms saying it.

A thought B said:

1. he/she was Welsh.
2. his/her father was the chairman of the Board.
3. he/she was engaged to a member of the Royal Family.
4. he/she came by train.
5. his wife/her husband was a TV producer.
6. he/she spoke German fluently.

h) How to reply by denying or correcting what was said

No,	I didn't(, actually). not to my knowledge. I don't believe I did. I don't think so.	(I've never even been to Brighton.)
No, what I said was (that)		I was thinking of getting married. my mother lived there. I liked the name Charles. I lived in Brightling. my brother was one. you couldn't see me on Friday.

PRACTICE 6

Work in pairs. A asks questions seeking confirmation, using the situations below. B denies ever having said it, using the words in brackets.

A thought that B said:

1. he/she was divorced. *(I'm not even married.)*
2. he/she lived in Chelsea. *(I don't even live in London.)*
3. his/her mother was an artist. *(My mother's never painted a thing in her life.)*
4. he/she was a friend of Paul McCartney. *(I've never even heard of him.)*
5. his/her ambition was to be a lion-tamer. *(I'm terrified of dogs, let alone lions.)*
6. he/she played the piano. *(I can't play any instrument.)*

PRACTICE 7

Work in pairs. A asks questions seeking confirmation, using the situations below. B corrects A, using the words in brackets.

A thought that B said:

1. he/she was Irish. *(My boyfriend/girlfriend was.)*
2. his/her father owned a restaurant. *(My father worked in one.)*
3. he/she came from Scotland. *(My ancestors did.)*
4. his/her boss was here. *(I was glad he wasn't here.)*
5. he/she was having a party on Saturday. *(I wanted to go to one on Saturday.)*
6. He'd/she'd written a novel. *(If I had the time I'd write one.)*

Unit 14: Asking For and Giving Information (2)

i) How to ask for a statement to be repeated

There are many occasions when you have to ask someone to repeat a statement. Here are some phrases you can use:

> A: By the way, where did you go for your holidays this year?
> B: Blakeney.

Sorry? Pardon?	Where did you say you went? Where did you go?	
Sorry, I'm afraid	I didn't (quite)	hear what you said. get that.
Could you	repeat it? say it again?	
What did you say? Where (was it)?		
I beg your pardon?	Where did you say?	

PRACTICE 8

Work in pairs. A asks a question and B answers. A then follows up with another question asking B to repeat his/her answer. Use the situations below. But first look at the example.

e.g. You went to Blakeney for your holiday this year. *(Where?)* It's a small town in Norfolk.

> A: By the way, where did you go for your holidays this year?
> B: Blakeney.
> A: *Sorry? Where did you say you went?*
> B: Blakeney. It's a small town in Norfolk.
> A: Oh, I see.

1. You went to Horam at the weekend. *(Where?)* It's a small village in Sussex.
2. John lost a plectrum at the party. *(What?)* It's something you use when you play the guitar.
3. You are all meeting outside the station at 19.30. *(When?)* That's 7.30 p.m.
4. The girl James is talking to is Fiona Simple-Smooth. *(Who?)* Her father owns the Grand Hotel.
5. It will take two weeks to get the films developed. *(How long?)* They have to be sent away to Oxford.

j) How to follow up a person's answer by asking for further details

e.g. You have applied for a job as hotel manager at a large London hotel.

> A: Tell me, where did you last work?
> B: At a hotel in Hastings.
> A: I see.

But	which hotel,	(exactly,)	(was it)?
	what		did you do there?
	what job,		did you do?

But	perhaps you could be a little more specific.
	I need to know a little bit more about the hotel.
	could you give me further details about your job.

Which hotel, Where		was it?
What	(exactly,)	did you do?
I wonder if you could tell me what		your job was?

155

Unit 14: Asking For and Giving Information (2)

PRACTICE 9

Work in pairs. A asks a question and B answers. A then follows up B's answer by asking for further details. Use the situations below. But first look at the example.

e.g. You last worked at a hotel in Hastings. *(Where?)* You were a waiter. *(What?)*

> A: Tell me, where did you last work?
> B: At a hotel in Hastings.
> A: I see. *But what exactly did you do there?*
> B: I was a waiter.
> A: Oh, I see.

1. You last worked at a school in Kent. *(Where?)* You taught English and Drama. *(What?)*
2. You learned to speak English at a language school in London. *(Where?)* It was the Royal School of English in Kensington. *(Which?)*
3. You work at the B.B.C. *(Where?)* You are a Production Assistant. *(What?)*
4. John is writing a book at the moment. *(What?)* It's a novel about big business. *(What sort?)*
5. Christine is away because she's in hospital. *(Why?)* She's got pneumonia. *(What?)*
6. You want to leave your present job because it's boring. *(Why?)* It's boring because you do the same thing day in and day out. *(In what way?)*

k) How to follow up an answer by expressing surprise

e.g. You have applied for a job as hotel manager at a large London hotel.

> A: And which other hotels have you worked at?
> B: None, actually.
> A: Oh!

| But | how can you possibly / how, on earth, do you | expect to | get this job |

if you haven't worked at a hotel before?

| So you haven't | really / actually | had any experience of hotel work?

PRACTICE 10

Work in pairs. A asks a question and B answers, using the situations below. The answer is unexpected and A follows it up with a question expressing surprise.

1. You want to borrow a friend's car.
   He didn't know you had passed your driving test and asks when you did so. You haven't passed it. *(borrow my car if you haven't passed your test)*
2. You have applied for a part in a television play.
   The producer wants to know which other TV plays you've been in. You have never been on television before. *(had any experience of working on television)*
3. You have applied for a job in Germany.
   The interviewer wants to know how well you speak German. You don't speak it at all. *(get a job in Germany without knowing the language)*
4. You are talking about Richard Burton with some friends, and you say he's a terrible actor.
   Someone asks you which films you have seen him in. You haven't seen any. *(seen him act)*
5. You are going to work in Britain.
   A friend asks you if you've got a work permit. You were refused one. *(work in Britain without a work permit)*
6. You tell someone you intend to get married at Christmas.
   He/she asks who you are going to marry. You don't know yet. *(found anyone, then)*

Unit 14: Asking For and Giving Information (2)

Dialogue

Practise reading the following dialogue in pairs. Read the dialogue again, replacing the phrases in **bold** with phrases of similar meaning. Then write out the new dialogue.

A: Now, **would you mind telling me** why you applied for this job?

B: Well, my present job is very boring and...

A: **Perhaps you could be a little more specific. In what way exactly is it boring?**

B: Well, I just sit at a desk all day, more or less doing the same thing.

A: And **do you think this job will be more interesting?**

B: Yes, I do. In fact, this is the main reason why I applied for it.

A: Yes, I see...
   I hope you don't mind me asking this but you haven't been in trouble with the police at any time, have you?

B: Oh, no! Well, I was caught speeding once.

A: **Sorry? I didn't quite hear what you said.** You were what?

B: I was caught speeding.

A: Oh! **Was it recently?**

B: No, it wasn't. It was six or seven years ago, in fact.

A: That's good...
　　Now, **I wonder if you could tell me** how much experience you've had of selling things?

B: **Did you say experience?**

A: Yes, that's right.

B: Well, I...

A: Yes?

B: I... I've never actually sold anything in my life.

A: What? **But how can you possibly expect to** get this job if you've never done any selling before?

B: Well, I didn't think it mattered very much. I thought I'd get some sort of training here.

A: Oh, you did, did you?...

Written Practice

Complete the following dialogues:

1. A: .... why you applied for this job?
   B: ....

2. A: .... but you're not really going to marry Fiona, are you?
   B: .... *(gives a direct answer)*

3. A: .... but you are wearing a wig, aren't you?
   B: .... *(refuses or evades answering)*

4. A: .... you were a dancer, ...?
   B: No, ... that *(corrects what was said)*

5. A: By the way, ... at the weekend?
   B: Llanelli.
   A: .... *(asks the person to repeat his answer)*

Unit 14: Asking For and Giving Information (2)

6. A: Tell me, ... work when you first left school?
   B: In a factory.
   A: I see. But .... *(asks for further details)*

7. A: And what other languages do you speak apart from English?
   B: None, actually.
   A: Oh! But .... get this job as an interpreter if you only speak English.

8. A: And how do you find working with children?
   B: I don't know. I've only worked with adults.
   A: Oh! So .... had any experience of working with children?

Role-Play

APPLYING FOR A SUMMER JOB

Work in pairs. Look at the following advertisement:

Summer Vacancies

Can't afford to go on holiday this summer? Then why not combine a holiday with a job? Come and work at one of our holiday camps in Eastbourne, Cornwall, Blackpool, Wales, Scotland or the Isle of Man.

Vacancies exist for the following:

- entertainers
- barmen/barmaids
- kitchen assistants
- cleaners
- waiters/waitresses
- sports leaders
- nursery assistants

Send immediately for application form to:
HIGH-LIFE HOLIDAYS
Box No. 347

Person A is an interviewer, while Person B is someone looking for a job during the summer. Person B fills in the application form on page 161 and gives it to Person A.

Before starting the interview, read through the notes on page 184 (Person A) and page 189 (Person B). When you are both ready, the interview can begin.

When you have done it once, change roles and do it again.

Unit 14: Asking For and Giving Information (2)

HIGH-LIFE HOLIDAYS
204 Regent's Drive
London EC1V 7NU

APPLICATION FORM

Job required: ....

Full name: ....

Address: ....

Date of birth: .... Tel. No: ....

Married/Single/Divorced

Holiday Camp: 1st choice: .... 2nd Choice: ....

Dates: From: .... to: ....

Present job: ....

Previous jobs: ....
....
....
....

Education after age of 11: *School:* ....
University: ....

Hobbies and interests: ....
....
....

Other information: ....
....
....
....

Signature: .... Date: ....

Unit 15: Future Plans and Intentions

Brian and Peter are talking about the summer holidays.

BRIAN: I don't know if you've heard, Peter, but some of us are thinking of going to Brighton in the summer. I don't know if you've made your holiday plans yet, but if not perhaps you'd like to come with us?

PETER: Well, that's very kind of you, Brian, but it's a bit difficult to say at the moment. When are you thinking of going?

BRIAN: Oh, some time in July. Around about the 16th, I think.

PETER: I see. And for how long – a fortnight?

BRIAN: Well, we were going to but now one or two of the other students say they can't afford it, so it'll just be a week. You're interested, then?

PETER: Oh yes – very much, but the problem is that Sally only gets two weeks' holiday in the summer. And we usually go to Italy. It all depends when she gets her holidays, really.

BRIAN: I see. When do you think you'll know for certain?

PETER: Oh, it should be quite soon, I think. But providing it's the same time then we'd love to come.

BRIAN: That's good. It should be fun.

PETER: Do you know how much it's going to cost?

BRIAN: Yes – about £50 altogether.

PETER: Oh, that's quite reasonable. Is everybody going?

BRIAN: Yes, most of them. Not Gloria, of course. She's off to the Bahamas again.

PETER: Lucky thing! It must be nice to have parents living abroad.

BRIAN: Yes, it must. But supposing you had a lot of money, Peter, where would you like to go for a holiday?

PETER: Oh, I'd probably go to America, or Japan maybe. Somewhere far away, anyway. And you?

BRIAN: I don't know really. Perhaps a world cruise.

PETER: Yes, that would be fantastic.

BRIAN: Anyway, I can put your name down, then. Provisionally, at least?

PETER: Yes, please. And I'll let you know definitely the minute I hear from Sally.

BRIAN: Fine.

The Royal Pavilion, Brighton

Unit 15: Future Plans and Intentions

a) How to inquire about a person's future plans

When you want to ask someone about his/her future plans or intentions, here are some phrases you can use:

| What are you | going to
hoping to
planning to
intending to
proposing to
aiming to | do | (when you leave school)? |

| What do you | hope to
plan to
intend to
propose to
aim to
mean to | do | (when you leave school)? |

| What | do you think you'll
will you | do | (when you leave school)? |
| | are you thinking of | doing | |

b) How to state definite plans

| I'm | going to
planning to
intending to
proposing to
aiming to | (go to university). |
| | (going to university). | |

163

Unit 15: Future Plans and Intentions

I	plan to intend to propose to aim to mean to	(get a job somewhere).
I'll		

PRACTICE 1

Work in pairs. A asks B about his/her future plans or intentions, using the words below. B states a definite plan he/she has in mind.

1. what (do) after class
2. where (go) next summer
3. who (invite) to your party
4. when (move) to Scotland
5. what (do) at the weekend
6. when (get) married

c) How to state tentative plans

Well,	I'm hoping to I hope to I think I'll	(go to university).
	I'm thinking of	(going to university).

PRACTICE 2

Work in pairs. A asks B about his/her future plans or intentions, using the words below. B states a tentative plan he/she has in mind.

1. what (do) for a living
2. where (live) when you retire
3. when (move) into your new house
4. what (do) with the money your uncle left you
5. where (spend) Christmas
6. how many people (invite) to your wedding

d) How to state conditional plans

Well,	providing as long as if	(I pass my exams)	I'll	(go to university).

Unit 15: Future Plans and Intentions

PRACTICE 3

Work in pairs. A asks B about his/her future plans or intentions, using the situations below. B states his/her conditional plans. Try to ask and answer in as many different ways as possible.

1. At the moment you are at school. You want to go to university, but you have to pass your exams first.
2. You are on holiday next week. If you can afford it, you will go to Spain.
3. You have seen a house you would like to buy. But you cannot buy it without a mortgage.
4. You need a guest speaker for your annual dinner. You have asked Sir Harold Wilson and he has promised to try to postpone another engagement to be with you.
5. You are going to Spain next week. You want to lie on the beach all day and you hope that the weather will be nice.

PRACTICE 4

Look at the following table showing some of the problems facing the present Government, and the measures they plan or hope to take to overcome them.

PROBLEM	DEFINITE PLAN	TENTATIVE PLAN	CONDITIONAL PLAN
inflation	devalue the £	restrict imports	freeze wages if unions agree
lack of housing	give local authorities more money	give generous loans to private building contractors	release more land for building if the farmers agree
unemployment	subsidize key industries	give huge tax concessions to foreign investors	raise the school-leaving age to 17 if the costs are not too high
the price of food	bring in a general price freeze for 3 months	have a further 6-month period of intensified price monitoring	subsidize milk, cheese, bread and eggs, if the Common Market agrees
the increase in crime and violence	enlarge the police force by 20%	bring in harsher punishments, especially for first offenders	reintroduce the death penalty, if it can be got through Parliament

Unit 15: Future Plans and Intentions

Using the table, we can make up the following dialogue:

> A: What *are* the Government *going to* do about *inflation*?
> B: Well, to start with, they're *going* to *devalue the £*.
> A: Are they?
> B: Yes, and they're also *thinking of restricting imports*.
> A: Really?
> B: And I've also heard that they'll freeze wages, *providing the unions agree*.
> A: Well, that sounds encouraging. Do you think it will work?
> B: I don't know. But at least they're trying to do something about it.

Now practise making up further dialogues, based on the one above, about the Government's plans for other problems. Try to use as many different phrases as possible.

e) How to talk about changed plans or intentions

Occasionally, we make plans which for one reason or another we are forced to change. When you talk about your changed plans, here are some phrases you can use:

e.g. Are you going to Brighton at the weekend?

Well, I was	going to, planning to, intending to, hoping to, meaning to, thinking of doing it,	(but I can't now because there's something wrong with my car).

Well, I had	planned to, intended to, hoped to, meant to, thought of doing it,	(but I've changed my mind).

PRACTICE 5

Look at this dialogue:

> A: I thought Susan *was going to give up smoking*.
> B: Yes, she *was going to*, but she changed her mind.
> A: Oh! Why's that?
> B: Because she *found it too difficult*.

Work in pairs. Practise making up further dialogues, based on the above, using the words below. A asks a question. B answers, using the words shown in brackets. Change the verb where necessary. Try to use as many different phrases as possible.

1. You play golf with John (*he's not feeling very well*)
2. You go to Sally's party (*my sister's asked me to baby-sit for her*)
3. You take Doreen out for a meal (*we're not speaking to one another at the moment*)
4. You visit my cousin in Battle (*I can't really afford the train fare*)
5. You have a party at my place (*my parents have decided to come down for the weekend*)
6. You go to the concert (*it's been cancelled*)
7. Tom – teach in Sweden (*didn't want to leave his girlfriend*)
8. June – get married (*met someone else*)
9. Arthur – become an actor (*didn't think he was good enough*)
10. Your parents – move to Wales (*couldn't find a house they liked*)

PRACTICE 6

Look at the following:

> A: I thought you said the Government *were planning to reintroduce the death penalty*.
> B: Yes, they *had hoped to* but *they couldn't get it through Parliament*.

Now go back to Practice 4, and make up similar dialogues about the things the Government were planning or hoping to do, giving reasons why they were unable to do so.

Unit 15: Future Plans and Intentions

f) How to speculate about possible events

We often guess or speculate about the future.

e.g. You have applied for a job. Although there were more than a hundred applicants, you have a lot of experience and did fairly well in the interview. So it is possible that you will get the job.

In this case, someone could ask:

Tell me,	what will you do how will you feel	if	you get the job?

and you could answer:

Oh,	I suppose I expect I think I dare say I imagine I guess	I'll	go out and celebrate.
			be very happy indeed.
	I'll probably		

PRACTICE 7

Work in pairs. B imagines he/she is the person in the picture. A asks him/her questions using the words given. B says what he/she will do if the event happens.

1. if you pass your exam

3. if you lose your job

2. if you fail your exam

4. if you get promotion

Unit 15: Future Plans and Intentions

5. if you fail your driving test

7. if you win the race

6. if you pass your driving test

8. if you lose the race

g) How to speculate about unlikely or impossible events

Sometimes when we speculate about the future, we are day-dreaming.

e.g. You try the football pools every week. It is possible to win £250,000, but you have very little chance of doing so.

In this case, someone could ask:

Supposing Just suppose Imagine Let's say What if	you won £250,000 on the football pools.

What would you do (with the money)? What do you think you'd do? How would you feel? How do you think you'd feel?

and you could answer:

Well, if that	happened, were possible,	I suppose I expect I think I dare say I imagine I guess	I'd	give up working.
		I'd probably		be very happy indeed.

169

Unit 15: Future Plans and Intentions

PRACTICE 8

Work in pairs. A speculates about an unlikely or impossible event, using the words below. B says what he/she would do if the event happened. Change the verb and try to use as many different phrases as possible.

1. live until you were 150
2. inherit a farm
3. become Prime Minister
4. have the chance to go to the moon
5. never grow old
6. be able to foretell the future

Written Practice

Complete the following dialogues:

1. A: What .... next summer?
   B: .... (*definite plan*)

2. A: Where .... live when you get married?
   B: .... (*tentative plan*)

3. A: What .... do with that money you won?
   B: .... buy a new house if I can find one. (*conditional plan*)

4. A: .... to get married next year?
   B: Well, I .... but I can't now.
   A: Oh! Why's that?
   B: Because ....

5. A: I thought James .... move to Scotland?
   B: Yes, he .... but he changed his mind.
   A: Oh! Why's that?
   B: Because ....

6. A: Tell me, ... if you win on Saturday?
   B: Oh, ...

7. A: .... you were King/Queen of England?
   B: Well, if that ...., ...

Unit 15: Future Plans and Intentions

Dialogue

Practise reading the following dialogue in pairs. Read the dialogue again, replacing the phrases in **bold** with phrases of similar meaning. Then write out the new dialogue.

A: What **are you going to** do when you leave school?

B: Oh, **I plan to** go on to university. And you?

A: Yes, **I'm hoping to** go to university, too. Well ... **providing** I pass my exams, of course.

B: But I thought you said you **were going to** get a job?

A: Yes, **I had planned to,** but I changed my mind.

B: Oh! Why's that?

A: Because there just aren't any jobs going at the moment – at least, not unskilled ones.

B: Yes, it's a problem all right. But **supposing** you could have any job in the world. Which one would you choose?

A: Well, if **that were possible, I think I'd** like to be a famous writer.

B: Oh? Any particular reason you'd choose that?

A: Not really, except that it must be nice seeing your name in print.

Magdalen College, Oxford

Future Plans and Intentions

Role-Play

SITUATION 1: MODERNIZING AN OLD COTTAGE

Work in pairs.

Each pair imagine they have bought an old cottage in Cornwall. They got it very cheaply (only £4,000) for the following reasons:

1. It has not been lived in for ten years.
2. The garden is overgrown (and quite large).
3. The roof needs re-thatching.
4. The rooms are small, dark and need to be redecorated.
5. There is no bathroom, only an outside lavatory, at the bottom of the garden.
6. There is no central heating and only one fireplace.
7. The stairs are unsafe in places and some of the windows are broken.
8. The whole cottage needs rewiring.
9. The kitchen only has a very large, cracked sink.
10. There is no garage.

Each pair want to modernize the cottage before moving in and are planning what jobs need to be done, and in which order they should be done. They also plan which jobs they can do themselves (at weekends) and which ones will have to be done by an expert.

Rock Stoppard

aged 32, pop singer

Sudden rise to fame two years ago with hit song: 'I used to kiss her on the lips – but it's all over now.' Now the biggest pop star in the world. Very wealthy. Has houses in California (where he lives), Ireland, the South of France and Sussex.

Married before to writer Marjorie Drab who was tragically killed in a car accident two years ago. One son, aged nine.

Samantha Crowbridge-Willett

aged 20 fashion model

Youngest daughter of the Earl of Wessex. Family estate near Tunbridge Wells. Expensive education. Became a model eighteen months ago and is quickly becoming world-famous. Labelled as the next 'Twiggy'.

Once tipped to marry the Prince of Wales. Engaged last year to actor Richard Bolton. Broke it off when she met Rock.

SITUATION 2: WHAT A WEDDING IT'S GOING TO BE!

Work in groups of four or five.

One person is Rock Stoppard and one person is Samantha Crowbridge-Willett. The others are gossip columnists for various newspapers. The journalists interview the couple about their wedding, future plans and anything else they may be interested in.

When both the couple and the gossip columnists are ready, they can begin the interview.

Before starting, the couple read through the notes on page 185, while the gossip columnists read through the notes on pages 189–90.

...ure Plans and Intentions

...TION 3: WHAT A CHOICE!

...in pairs.
...ach pair is given one of the following situations to look at:

> 1. Supposing atomic war has just broken out, and you have only ten minutes to get from your house/flat to the nearest air-raid shelter. Which things would you take with you?
> 2. Just suppose you won £500,000 in a competition, but the condition of the prize is that you have to spend all the money in one day, and that you must not spend more than £50,000 on any one single item. What would you buy?
> 3. What if you were told by your doctor that you only had one week left to live? How would you spend your last week?
> 4. Imagine you were able to change places with anyone in the world, living or dead, for one day. Who would you choose and why?
> 5. Let's say you were given three wishes – all of which would come true. What would you wish for?

Each pair work out what they would do if the particular situation they have been given happened, or were possible.

When each pair are ready, one person tells the rest of the class what they decided. The rest of the class can be asked for their comments.

Materials for Exercises and Role-Plays

Part 1: Role-Plays (whole group)
Unit 1: Role-Play (page 15)

Those meeting someone at the airport

ROLE 1

Your surname is Brooks. You work for the London branch of a Danish travel agency. You are meeting someone called Hansen who recently won a competition run by your travel agency in Denmark. (The prize was a week's holiday in London!) You have a car waiting to take him/her to his/her hotel.

ROLE 2

Your name is Pauline (or Peter) Young. You are meeting someone from America called Jonathan (or Samantha) Williams. You have been a pen-pal with him/her for over two years. But this is the first time you have ever met and you are feeling a bit nervous. Your car is in the car park.

ROLES 3 AND 3a

Your name is Simon (or Julie) Jones (Role 3). You are meeting your cousin from Australia, Susan (or Brian) Fleming. He/she has come to England for a holiday. You haven't seen him/her for more than fifteen years, so you are not sure whether you will recognize him/her. Your fiancé(e) is with you (Role 3a). You will catch a train back to your parents' house.

ROLE 4

Your surname is Black. You are the sales manager of an electrical company. You are meeting someone called Ott. He/she comes from Austria and you are hoping to do business with his/her company. You have a car waiting to take him/her to his/her hotel.

ROLE 5

Your surname is Lake. You are an editor. You work for a British publishing company. You are meeting a famous Canadian writer, Claudia (or Steve) Bellow. Your company is hoping to publish some of his/her books. You will get a taxi back to London and you are really looking forward to taking him/her out for a meal tonight. (You have booked a table at one of the best restaurants in London!)

Those being met at the airport

ROLE 1

Your surname is Hansen. You are Danish. You recently won a competition in a newspaper – the first prize being a week's holiday in London. You have just arrived from Copenhagen. The flight was very rough and you have a headache. Someone from the travel agency that ran the competition is meeting you at the airport.

ROLE 2

Your name is Jonathan (or Samantha) Williams. You have flown from New York to London to meet someone called Pauline (or Peter) Young. You have been a pen-pal with him/her for more than two years, but this is the first time you have ever met. You are really looking forward to meeting him/her and to seeing London. You are also a bit tired after the long flight.

ROLE 3

Your name is Susan (or Brian) Fleming. You have flown to England from Australia. You have come here for a holiday and to visit relatives. You are being met at Heathrow by one of your cousins – someone called Simon (or Julie). You haven't seen him/her since your family emigrated to Australia fifteen years ago. The journey was long but pleasant. (You saw two very good films on the plane.) You have a lot of luggage with you.

ROLE 4

Your surname is Ott. You live in Austria. You have flown to London from Vienna on business. Your firm is hoping to do business with a British electrical company. You are being met at the airport by their sales manager – someone called Black. The flight was very smooth and you are looking forward to visiting London again.

ROLES 5 AND 5a

You are Claudia (or Steve) Bellow (Role 5). You are a famous Canadian writer. You have flown from Vancouver to London to meet the editor of a British publishing company which is interested in publishing some of your books. His/her name is Lake. Your husband (or wife) is with you (Role 5a). He/she wanted to come along to do some shopping in London. The flight was very tiring and you are both looking forward to an early night.

Materials for Exercises and Role-Plays

Unit 2: Group Work (page 27)

'Find out' cards

Find out: **1**

1. who can do a handstand.
2. who grew up in a small village.
3. whose favourite sport is football.
4. who doesn't like pop music.
5. who is going abroad for his/her holidays next summer.
6. who walked to school today.

Find out: **2**

1. who can touch his/her toes.
2. who has more than two brothers and sisters.
3. who knows the opposite of the word 'voluntary'. (*compulsory*)
4. who thinks English is a difficult language to learn.
5. who has moved recently.
6. who was born in December.

Find out: **3**

1. who can dance the tango.
2. who has a dog.
3. who knows what the capital of Wales is called. (*Cardiff*)
4. who in the group is older than you.
5. who hates getting up early.
6. who usually reads a daily newspaper.

Find out: **4**

1. who can raise one eyebrow.
2. who learnt German at school.
3. whose favourite colour is green.
4. who has been learning English for more than five years.
5. who is going home by bus today.
6. who thinks he/she is shy.

Find out: **5**

1. who can skate backwards.
2. who has been to Scotland.
3. who was born in the same month as you were.
4. who is afraid of spiders.
5. who wants to be a millionaire.
6. who is left-handed.

Find out: **6**

1. who can play the piano or the guitar.
2. who went to bed after 10.30 last night.
3. who has a boyfriend/ girlfriend.
4. who has read an English novel recently.
5. who likes doing homework.
6. who prefers cats to dogs.

Find out: **7**

1. who is an uncle or an aunt.
2. who knows how to play chess.
3. who has visited Paris.
4. who can wink (with both eyes).
5. who doesn't have any brothers or sisters.
6. who went abroad last summer for his/her holidays.

Find out: **8**

1. who wants to get married and have children one day.
2. who prefers tea to coffee.
3. who can remember what the weather was like this time last week.
4. who was born in May or April.
5. who is more than six months younger than you are.
6. who is interested in history.

Materials for Exercises and Role-Plays

Unit 7: Role-Play (page 83)

PERSON A

You have a large flat in Tottenham. You do not really want to use it, because you are afraid that something will get broken. Also your landlady lives on the bottom floor and she does not like parties to go on longer than 11.30 p.m. You have lots of records and you are prepared to take them to the party. But you hate cooking and washing up. You would like to bring your boyfriend/girlfriend.

PERSON B

You have a small flat in Chelsea. You think the party should be for your class only and that everyone should help equally. You are prepared to do everything except move furniture. You also think it would be better to buy food than to make it. During the discussion, you will make notes of what everyone offers to do, plus any other decisions that are made.

PERSON C

You share a large flat in Knightsbridge. You do not mind using it for the party, but if you do then you would have to invite the two people you share the flat with. In fact, you think the more people who are invited the better the party will be. You would also prefer to buy plastic spoons, knives, cups etc. instead of everyone bringing their own. It would also mean no washing up! You do not like cooking very much and think it might be cheaper to buy something from a 'take-away' restaurant.

PERSON D

You live with your family in Fulham. You do not think they would mind you using their house for the party, but, of course, they would have to be invited too. You do not really want to do anything except bring records, so you keep finding excuses for not helping. You do not mind whether other people are invited to the party or not, but you think there should be equal numbers of males and females.

PERSON E

You have quite a large flat in Bayswater. You do not mind using it for the party but the only problem is that you don't have a record-player. You love organizing things and tend to 'take over' a discussion and boss people about. You do not mind helping with everything but feel that the cooking, washing up etc. should be left to the men.* You would like to invite some friends who are visiting London at the moment.
(NOTE: *If this role is played by a man, change 'men' to 'women'.)

Unit 9: Role-Play (page 98)

PERSON A

This is your problem. When you phone up about it, try to put it in your own words. (Do not just read it out!)

You have invited your girlfriend's/boyfriend's parents over to your flat for a meal at the weekend. This is the first time you have invited them for a meal, and you want to make a good impression. You are not a very good cook and wonder if the panel could suggest something you could make – something which isn't too difficult, but something which will impress them. (Your girlfriend/boyfriend has offered to help you, but you want to do it alone.)

PERSON B

This is your problem. When you phone up about it, try to put it in your own words. (Do not just read it out!)

You are an au-pair in this country. Because you are very shy and because your English is not very good you have found it difficult to make friends. You have been here three months, but don't really know anyone apart from the family you work for. You would like to know if the panel could suggest where you could go to meet people and also if they know any ways of overcoming your shyness.

PERSON C

This is your problem. When you phone up about it, try to put it in your own words. (Do not just read it out!)

You are married and your problem is your mother-in-law. When her husband died, she was very upset and came to live with you for a while to 'get over it'. But that was two years ago! And it doesn't look as if she will ever leave now. The problem is that she interferes all the time – telling you and your wife/husband how to look after the children, the home, and so on. You have tried talking to your wife/husband about her, but he/she just tells you to wait a bit longer. Unfortunately, you can't and are now thinking of either leaving your wife/husband or else telling your mother-in-law she isn't welcome any more. You would like to know what the panel would suggest you do.

PERSON D

This is your problem. When you phone up about it, try to put it in your own words. (Do not just read it out!)

Materials for Exercises and Role-Plays

Your problem is the family next door. They moved in three months ago and since then you've had nothing but trouble. To begin with, they have a big dog which keeps coming into your garden and destroying your flowers. When you complained about this, your neighbour told you to make your fence stronger. They seem to have a lot of parties during the week, which go on very late and are so noisy that it's impossible to sleep. When you complained to your neighbour he told you to join in the party instead. But the final straw was last week when your son was attacked by the neighbours' two children on the way home from school. He was quite badly hurt and is now afraid of walking past their house. You've had enough. You don't want to move but you also can't go on living next door to such people. You wonder if the panel can give you some advice.

Part 2: Role-Play/Exercise Materials
Person A

Unit 4: Role-Play (page 43)

PAIRS

You want to go somewhere this weekend with a friend (Person B). Look through the Weekend Guide on page 44 and try to find somewhere suitable. You like animals, flowers and looking at exhibitions. You do not like sport.

You can begin: **Shall we go somewhere this weekend?**

GROUPS OF THREE

You want to go somewhere this weekend with two friends (Persons B and C). Look through the Weekend Guide on page 44 and try to find somewhere suitable. You like football, animals and photography. You would like to go somewhere on both Saturday and Sunday. You are not very keen on exhibitions.

You can begin: **Shall we go somewhere this weekend?**

Unit 6: Role-Play (page 73)

You are a sales manager. You phone up Person B, who is the chief buyer of a firm you do business with, to arrange a meeting some time next week. Try to find a suitable day and time, even if it means rearranging your plans. Here is your diary for next week:

	morning	afternoon
Monday	visit new warehouse 10.30	free
Tuesday	meet directors 11.15	dental appointment 2.30
Wednesday	free	job interviews
Thursday	show visitor round factory	free
Friday	board meeting 9.30	fly to Paris 2.30

Materials for Exercises and Role-Plays

Unit 13: Role-Play (page 147)

ROLE-PLAY 1

Your surname is Gardener. You are waiting at the bus stop when your neighbour, Mr/Mrs Green, comes along. It's a very windy day. Ask about his/her daughter, Julie, who got married a few weeks ago. Your own family are well, except for your wife/husband, who has just lost his/her job. There's a rumour going around that Mrs Spratt from Number 34 is in hospital. You want to know if Mr/Mrs Green knows anything about it.

ROLE-PLAY 2

Your name is David (or Sally) Cramp. You are cutting the front lawn when a friend of yours, Charlie (or Joan) Spratt, walks past. It's a sunny day. Ask about his wife/her husband, who, the last time you saw him/her, was in hospital. Your own family are all well, and your daughter, Claire, has just had twins! You heard from Billy Watson that the Regal Cinema was going to be pulled down after Christmas and want to know if Charlie (or Joan) has heard anything about it.

Unit 14: Role-Play (page 160)

1. While Person B is filling in his/her application form, try to think of some general questions you can ask, e.g.

   > if he's/she's ever been to or worked at a holiday camp before his/her present job
   > why he/she wants this job

2. When you receive Person B's application form, you may be able to work out further questions from it.
3. You will also be expected to be able to give information about the following:

   > what the job entails (i.e. what the person will be expected to do)
   > the pay
   > the working hours
   > the amount of free time
   > accommodation

4. When you have finished the interview, tell Person B that you will inform him/her next week whether he's/she's got the job.

Materials for Exercises and Role-Plays

Unit 15: Role-Play (page 173)

Situation 2: the couple

1. Read carefully through the background notes.
2. The journalists will ask you lots of questions. These may be about the following:

The wedding	– where/when it's going to be; number of guests; reception; best man; bridesmaids etc.
The honeymoon	– where you plan to go; for how long?; reasons for choosing this place etc.
Future plans	– where you intend to live; both work?; children? etc.

3. Of course, they may want to know other things, e.g.

where you met
if it was love at first sight
how you proposed
where it was

So be prepared to use your imagination!

Materials for Exercises and Role-Plays

Person B

Unit 1: Practice 2 (page 9)

1. Your name is Brown (Person B). Someone is meeting you at the airport (Person A). Your girlfriend/boyfriend is with you (Person C). His/her name is Tom/Gloria.
2. Your name is Green (Person B). Someone is meeting you at the airport (Person A). Your son/daughter is with you (Person C). His/her name is John/Pauline.
3. Your name is Owen (Person B). Someone is meeting you at the station (Person A). Your business colleague is with you (Person C). His/her name is Roger/Rita Nestles.
4. Your name is Carroll (Person B). Someone is meeting you at the station (Person A). Your secretary is with you (Person C). His/her name is James/Barbara Sharpe.
5. Your name is Davies (Person B). Someone called Collins is meeting you at the airport (Person A). Your husband/wife is with you (Person C). His/her name is Gerald/Josephine.
6. Your name is Smooth (Person B). Someone called Steadman is meeting you at the airport (Person A). Your partner is with you (Person C). His/her name is Michael/Margaret Blake.

Unit 3: Role-Play (page 36)

Situation 1

You have applied for a job at Anytown library. Your interview is tomorrow. You phone up the library to ask how to get there from the station. Person A works at the library. Listen to the directions he/she gives you, then mark in your route on the map on page 187.

Situation 2

You have driven down to Anytown from London to visit your grandmother, who is in hospital. You stop your car opposite All Saints church and ask someone who is standing there (Person A) the way to the hospital. Listen to the directions he/she gives you, then mark in your route on the map on page 187.

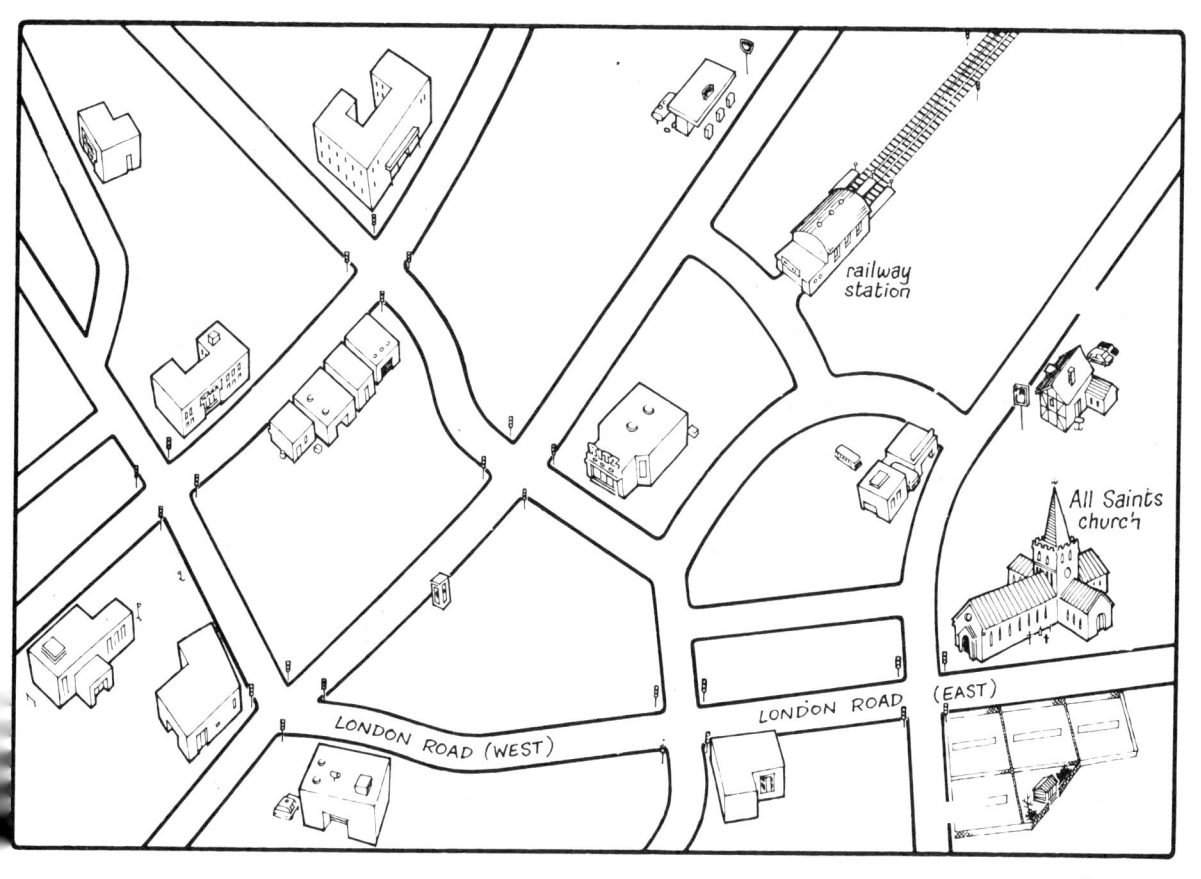

Anytown

Unit 4: Role-Play (page 43)

PAIRS

You want to go somewhere this weekend with a friend (Person A). Look through the Weekend Guide on page 44 and try to find somewhere suitable. You love sport, photography and looking at historic buildings. But you do not like exhibitions very much.

GROUPS OF THREE

You want to go somewhere this weekend with two friends (Persons A and C). Look through the Weekend Guide on page 44 and try to find somewhere suitable. You do not really mind where you go but you would prefer somewhere indoors in case the weather is bad. You have heard that the Ideal Home Exhibition at the Town Hall is really worth seeing.

Materials for Exercises and Role-Plays

Unit 6: Role-Play (page 73)

Situation 1

You are the chief buyer of a manufacturing company. You receive a phone call from the sales manager of a company you often do business with (Person A). He/she wants to see you some time next week. Try to find a suitable day and time to see him/her, even if it means rearranging your plans. Here is your diary for next week:

	morning	afternoon
Monday	free	see sales manager 2.30
Tuesday	see bank manager 10.30	board meeting 1.15
Wednesday	go to Birmingham 8.30	attend conference
Thursday	return to London 11.10	play golf 2 p.m.
Friday	go over new plans	free

Situation 2

You receive a phone call from Person A, who wants you to have dinner at his/her flat one evening next week. However, you don't really like him/her very much, so you try to find excuses for not accepting the invitation.

Unit 13: Role-Play (page 147)

ROLE-PLAY 1

Your surname is Green. You see your neighbour, Mr/Mrs Gardener, waiting at the bus stop. Stop and have a chat. The weather is terrible. Ask about his/her family and if it's true that his wife/her husband has lost his/her job. Your own family are fine – especially your daughter, Julie, who got married recently. They're going to buy a new house in Grove Road. You can't talk for long because you have a lot of shopping to do.

Materials for Exercises and Role-Plays

ROLE-PLAY 2

Your name is Charlie (or Joan) Spratt. You see a friend of yours, David (or Sally) Cramp, cutting his/her front lawn. Stop and have a chat. The weather is beautiful and you've heard that it's going to stay like this for another week. Ask about his/her family. Yours are all right except for your husband/wife, who has just come out of hospital and still isn't very well. You are on your way to the chemist's to get some medicine for him/her, so you can't stay very long.

Unit 14: Role-Play (page 160)

1. Decide which job you would like to apply for, then fill in the application form on page 161. You can use your own background or you can make one up. (Remember to make a brief note of what you have put down on your application form.)
2. When you have finished, hand the form to Person A.
3. During the interview you will have a chance to ask questions. Here are some things you could think about:

> what you will have to do
> number of hours per week
> the pay
> the amount of free time
> the accommodation offered

You may be able to think of other things to ask.

Unit 15: Role-Play (page 173)

Situation 2: gossip columnists

1. Read through the background notes about the couple.
2. Prepare a list of questions to ask the couple. You can ask about:

(a) *their plans*, e.g.

> When/where are you getting married?
> How many guests do you plan to invite?
> Where will you hold the reception?
> Who is going to be best man/bridesmaid?
> Do you plan to have a honeymoon? Where?
> Why did you choose this place?
> Are you both intending to go on working after you're married?
> Where do you plan to live?
> Are you thinking of having children?

(b) *other questions*, e.g.

> Where/when did you first meet?
> Was it love at first sight?
> How did Rock propose to you?

Think of other questions to ask.

Person C
Unit 1: Practice 2

See page 186.

Unit 4: Role-Play (page 43)

You would like to go somewhere this weekend with two friends (Persons A and B). Look through the Weekend Guide on page 44 and try to find somewhere suitable. You would quite like to go somewhere for a change – possibly a coach tour. You are also keen on sport, especially athletics. You have heard from your brother that the computer exhibition at the Trade Centre is really fascinating.

Acknowledgements

The Publisher wishes to thank the following for their kind permission to reproduce copyright photographic material: British Airways, p. 14; British Tourist Authority, pp. 7, 16, 26, 28, 37, 42, 45, 50, 51, 58, 62, 64, 72, 74, 88, 90, 99, 104, 106, 108, 114, 117, 129, 131, 155, 156, 158, 162, 171, 172; Camera Press, pp. 115, 173; Fox Photos Ltd, pp. 33, 108, 146; The Metropolitan Police, p. 148; 20th Century-Fox, p. 84.

The Publisher also wishes to thank the London Evening Standard for the Flat Buyers Guide, p. 92; and the Scottish Tourist Board for permission to reproduce the advertisements on page 60.